Parks for People

**BEN WHITAKER
and
KENNETH BROWNE**

Central Park: 840 acres in the middle of New York

PARKS

FOR

PEOPLE

SCHOCKEN BOOKS • NEW YORK

First SCHOCKEN PAPERBACK edition 1973

© 1971 Ben Whitaker and Kenneth Browne
Introduction copyright © 1973 by Schocken Books Inc.
Published by arrangement with Winchester Press
Library of Congress Catalog Card No. 73-81383
Manufactured in the United States of America

CONTENTS

Introduction

For some Americans one of the most important aspects of Ben Whitaker and Kenneth Browne's engaging book will be the Anglo-American environmental perspective of its English authors. This is understandable, for England remains in both myth and fact the source of most of the fundamental values and institutions that have shaped this country. And, it is important to note, this influence extended beyond the colonial inheritance of a common language and a common law to include a shared tradition of land planning and design that matured in the nineteenth century. Nor has the United States, as the authors realize, been a passive partner in this relationship. For example, it was the English experience with urban public parks in the first half of the nineteenth century that the United States adapted; and in the second half of that century American national parks influenced English planners. At various social, cultural, economic, and political levels, therefore, an interchange of environmental ideas, styles, and institutions has been maintained at least since the Victorian Age. The enduring contribution of this book is the authors' popular translation of the forms of this tradition—that is, shape, views, and composition of natural materials within the park—into the various social, ecological, and management processes by which successful designs are created and sustained.

The book has special meaning for those concerned with American cities. Whitaker and Browne were encouraged by the changes they observed in New York City, where "in 1965 a successful revolution was launched in the parks." They applaud, among other innovations, the closing of Central Park to automobiles on the weekends (a policy that has been extended to Prospect Park in Brooklyn and to Forest Park in Queens—and on other days) and the hiring-out of bicycles—an innovation that has had healthy effects not only on the park and its users but on the rest of the city as well, as bicycling has become for many an alternative to the automobile.

In addition, the authors note that Thomas Hoving, serving as the first park commissioner under Mayor John V. Lindsay, and Hoving's successor, August Heckscher, both were conscious of the lack of adequate recreational facilities in certain sections of the city. (Lindsay became co-chairman of the special Presidential commission charged with investigating the urban riots of the summer of 1967. The commission concluded that the absence of urban recreational facilities such as swimming pools was one cause of the resulting unrest.) Hence, it was sound social policy for both park commissioners to have "built new parks and sixty children's pools in the crowded slum areas [of New York City]." In short, one of the many lessons of the American urban experience in the 1960's was that open spaces—however visually attractive in themselves—are not separated slices of urban tissue; rather, they are inextricably related to the total life of the city.

Such an awareness is not new for many thoughtful Americans concerned with the state of their cities. Yet, it is useful to be reminded by England, where appreciation of urbane qualities has had a more enduring intellectual life. This urbanity is reflected in the maintenance and management of, for example, the public parks of London, Sheffield, and Birkenhead. Many Americans will recall the extent to which parks were considered the jewels of cities, offering multiple recreational opportunities as well as visual pleasure. And, of course, it is well to keep in mind that American cities vary considerably in their respective park policies. Urban centers such as Minneapolis, St. Paul, and Louisville appear to have much higher standards of preservation and maintenance than do New York, Boston, Buffalo, and Atlanta.

But it is difficult to discern anywhere in the United States today a municipal government or planning agency that is sufficiently aware, organizationally constituted, and adequately funded to be able to carry on the constant planning, design, and management of its open-space and recreational needs in terms of the comprehensive categories set forth in this book. Perhaps one of the implicit messages of this book is that such an urban land-planning policy requires the intervention of the national government to at least set standards of performance in the way that the national advisory commission on civil disorders provided guidance regarding urban social unrest. The development in England of the Peak District National park, which serves three urban conurbations, was inconceivable without national guidance.

Interestingly, the nucleus of such a policy did exist in the United States—particularly in New York City—during the nineteenth century. Central Park was planned and managed in the period 1858–1878 as a prototype for the rest of the country. As Whitaker and Browne indicate, the designers of that park, Frederick Law Olmsted and Calvert Vaux, did not work in isolation. They had the support of such prominent citizens as the editor William Cullen Bryant, the author Washington Irving, and the historian George Bancroft. In various ways these men reflected an understanding of the total meaning of open-space planning to the city. And, partly as a result of their efforts—although for a relatively brief time—there came into being a board of park commissioners with comprehensive powers over the planning of open spaces—including the streets. One of the still unwritten chapters of American urban history is the story of the conflict between those who continued to hold such views and their increasingly successful opponents, who represented land speculation, unbridled use of technology, and insensitivity to the multiple consequences of massive changes in the functions and needs of urban centers.

In a general way, the history of American urban open spaces can be viewed in terms of three general periods: 1850–1878, 1878–1920, and 1920–1964. This first period saw the flowering of a comprehensive Anglo-American environmental tradition. Although, as already noted, the political power needed to implement it was shortlived, such a tradition bolstered the forces responsible for creating many of the open spaces presently available in many cities. The debt which the present owes to the past—at least in terms of urban open spaces—is insufficiently recognized. The second period saw the gradual decline of this tradition—but not its extinction—to be replaced by a more aesthetically aggressive, but socially and ecologically impoverished, concern with the comprehensive conditions of urban life. It was during this time, too, that America experienced a new immigration from abroad, an increased movement of black people from the South into northern urban centers, and the introduction of that instrument of destruction to urban tissue— the automobile. And the third period, particularly the years since the end of World War II, witnessed a dramatic exodus from the South of black Americans and of Puerto Rican citizens from their island, and a movement of white middle-class citizens from the core city to surrounding suburbs. This last, the outward mass movement, was aided and abetted by the absence of a comprehensive land-use policy, the metastasis of the automobile, and an inter-related highway system.

This does not mean, of course, that American cities and suburbs ceased to acquire or plan for open spaces after 1878. But it does mean that their acquisition, planning, and maintenance—particularly in the twentieth century—was increasingly detached from comprehensive urban needs and from the awareness of the various social and ecological processes with which they intersect and on which their preservation and maintenance depend. The recollections many have of better park days can best be considered as temporary interludes before the realities of the national and urban condition caught up to the particular oasis that nourished these memories. As the inner cores of American cities decline, and as suburbs begin to exhibit precisely the same symptoms of environmental decay, popular attitudes regarding parks follow accordingly. It is a dreadful commentary on the popular state of mind, currently reflected in many American cities, that notwithstanding the complex environmental and urbane needs that parks serve, many today shun some of them either out of fear for personal safety or out of revulsion at their neglected condition. This is but a reflection of one of the current attitudes toward the inner city and some of the older suburbs.

PARKS FOR PEOPLE is not, however, a pessimistic book. Reflected on almost each page is the hope of remedying the faults of the past and of planning more adequately for the future. For example, the authors note how relatively few parks have been developed in most urban centers in recent times; that is, comprehensive planning of open spaces has tended to lag behind urban needs. In the United States much of the energy of those concerned with urban open spaces during recent times seems to have been expended upon the defense of what remains rather than upon finding ways to increase the amount and usefulness of park-land. And even where the original boundaries of a park may have been kept intact, large sections within it could have been misappropriated—as in Boston's Franklin Park, Buffalo's Delaware Park, and New York City's Central Park. Athletic stadia, golf courses, and adventure playgrounds all are important to urban dwellers, but their construction on what is already minimal and badly maintained parkland is a travesty of open-space usage.

In their chapter on "New Parks," Whitaker and Browne reflect the Anglo-American nineteenth-century optimism and genius for creating viable new open spaces out of seemingly "dead" or offensive urban land. They remind us, for example, that San Francisco's Golden Gate Park was created out of sand dunes, that the Backs at Cambridge, England, were constructed on rubble, and that Napoleon III, who was influenced by the English tradition of land-use planning and design, supported the masterly transformation of a sewage pit and abandoned gypsum works in Paris into Buttes-Chaumont Park. And, of course, almost every city in the world continues to have useless and even dangerous spaces within its limits, which could be converted to parkland.

Hence, this book is for everyone. Although the majority of the examples presented are drawn from the English and American experiences—with which the authors are most familiar—the book is truly international in scope. The urban open spaces of many different countries are referred to. Much of the compelling interest of Whitaker and Browne's presentation derives from their integration of this evidence into general trends applicable to all nations. "Before the end of this century," they write, "the forecast is that not only the population of the world is likely to double to 7,000 millions . . . but longevity and automation will mean that people in industrialized countries will have twice the amount of time for leisure than they have today." And during the same time, they warn, based upon present projections, there will be increasing appropriation of rural land for urban purposes, with little or no thought given to open spaces.

It is important to keep such major themes in mind while reading PARKS FOR PEOPLE, which is written with such enthusiasm and is so full of interesting data and recommendations that it would not be impossible—even given its summary chapter—to lose sight of the several larger points that give unity to the text. There are at least three points that give this work so much conceptual merit and which relate it to the Anglo-American environmental tradition out of which the authors are writing. The first is that public parks are basic to the health and welfare of any community. Well-planned open spaces, to which the authors point wherever they can, such as The Bos in Amsterdam, rather than being isolated physical designs, are critical to many different aspects of daily life. While shapes and forms may differ, the uses of open spaces are as basic to their users as the air they breathe. Indeed, the very quality of that air may be related to the quantity of open spaces available. The metaphor "lungs of the city," which persisted so long in many different dialects, reflects a popular international awareness of this still necessary function.

A second principal theme is the complexity of planning. Open spaces, whether defined as tot lots, adventure playgrounds, river-walks, or regional systems such as TVA contains, never just happen. They are always the result of interrelated social, cultural, economic, and political factors. And unless recognition of these factors is introduced into the planning of an open space, its future usefulness is placed in jeopardy. Similarly, it can be assumed that when open spaces function well, it is because adequate recognition has been given to the processes impinging on their operation and because the necessary specialists have been involved in their planning. Phrased differently, open spaces require the same care and thought in their planning, design, and management as any other complex physical and social units, such as schools, hospitals, and libraries.

The authors make this point in various ways. In their chapter on "Vandalism," for example, Whitaker and Browne refer to various sociological conclusions that indicate how vandalism can be diminished through careful planning and management. And in the same chapter they point to studies that demonstrate how improved recreational facilities contribute to the reduction of juvenile delinquency. But such studies relating social behavior to park design and management can only take place when the tradition of planning is expanded to include all aspects of open-space design. That such research is seldom conducted by municipal park agencies and such recom-

mendations rarely implemented attests to how divorced park planning remains from scientific study and analysis.

And the third theme relates to the aesthetics of parks—that is, the way they look to all who enjoy and appreciate beauty in the urban scene. It is, of course, true that to many the most obvious characteristic of open spaces is precisely their colorful contrast with the dense concrete masses surrounding them, and the juxtaposition of natural and manmade structures within them so as to create a particular set of scenes or views. It is not unusual—nor unreasonable—to compare the designing of an open space to the process of composing a landscape painting. Indeed, many, if not the majority, of landscape designers do consider themselves artists. And during the middle of the nineteenth century the American school and philosophy of landscape painting did influence the aesthetic of park planners such as Frederick Law Olmsted and Calvert Vaux. (Vaux's brother-in-law, for example, was the landscape painter Jervis McEntee.) There remain talented landscape designers such as Roberto Burle Marx, whose aesthetic images derive from a career in painting. Unquestionably, environmental artists have important roles to play in the planning and design of all open spaces. After all, *someone* has to give final shape to a project.

However, in the United States the balance between art and science in the planning process has been seriously upset since the end of the nineteenth century. As an integrated planning and design tradition declined, the myth of the great artist grew—at the expense of continued scientific study. The painting in a museum is dependent on scientific care with respect to its handling and the climatic control of the museum itself. When a painting is damaged, the process of restoration becomes more a matter of scientific study than of art. More importantly, the aesthetic of a park, unlike that of a painting, is composed of living materials that are more dependent on environmental influences than are paintings. These are materials that not only live and die—requiring replacement—but which have an unpredictable growth that is unique, producing an unplanned-for aesthetic—nature's own—which may be superior to and more exciting than anything "planned."

Another more obvious and critical difference that separates landscape design from the fine arts is that planned open spaces must accommodate a variety of different uses and large numbers of people whose presence has an impact on the aesthetic. In contrast to the scenes in many of the best landscape paintings of the nineteenth century, the landscapes of the park were meant to be populated; that is, people became part of the aesthetic. Also, the parks are planned primarily for various activities—they are not merely viewed from a distance—and such use has an effect on the life of the natural materials. Unless there is adequate planning, a mass gathering, for example, can damage the park physically as well as alter the aesthetic. The art of the landscape must be related to the science of the land and to its users.

This message is stressed throughout the book. The authors emphasize that landscape beauty is dependent on rational planning. "The squalor of our surroundings," they quote the noted English landscape architect Sylvia Crowe, "is due to the habit of separating beauty from the other aspects of life and looking upon it as an ornament to be indulged in on special occasions, instead of as a necessary and all-pervading quality." Whitaker and Browne have applied this principle—"that there should be no division between function and design"—to the book itself. Whitaker, a former member of the House of Commons, whose background is in the social sciences, wrote the text, while Browne, who is an artist, architect, and consultant in townscape design, supplied many of the ideas and illustrated the work. PARKS FOR PEOPLE, unlike many other illustrated works, reflects a truly cooperative and integrated approach.

Perhaps, then, the central message of the Anglo-American environmental perspective that flowered in both England and the United States in the mid-nineteenth century was the spirit of cooperation that existed between science and art as applied to the social improvement of urban populations. And since it was already clear by 1850 that urban centers would at some point be the chief containers of the majority of both nations, the health of cities was synonymous with the national welfare. If so, there is some reason to be optimistic that there has been taking place since the early 1960's in both countries a renaissance of the original comprehensive point of view that motivated distinguished landscape planners on both sides of the Atlantic more than a century ago. And this redefinition is occurring on at least three levels: the historical understanding of the tradition, theoretical definitions, and the establishment of centers of learning where this redefinition is being taught to future practitioners.

In nineteenth-century England the seminal figure of environmental planning and design was Sir Joseph Paxton, who made fundamental contributions to horticulture, architecture, land planning, and design. His plan for Birkenhead Park (1843) was one of the earliest efforts to create a new residential community for an industrial town; the plan incorporated the most advanced concepts of science and landscape art. But it was not until 1961 that George Chadwick published *The Works of Sir Joseph Paxton,* the first scholarly biography treating of Paxton's many environmental achievements. In 1966 Chadwick expanded his emphasis on Paxton's landscape work to include a historical and descriptive account of the public-park movements in the nineteenth and twentieth centuries (*The Park and the Town*). Since then Chadwick has moved away from historical studies into *A Systems View of Planning* (1971) in an effort to devise an integrated method of environmental analysis and action. England now has a degree-granting course of study in landscape architecture at the University of Sheffield under the chairmanship of Professor Arnold Weddle, whose concern is with an integration to environmental planning and design. A comprehensive approach is reflected in Weddle's work as a designer as well as educator.

This heightened environmental consciousness in England has paralleled efforts in the United States. For example, increased emphasis has been placed on the contribution of Frederick Law Olmsted. As the seminal environmental planner and designer of nineteenth-century America, Olmsted was deeply influenced by Paxton's work on Birkenhead, which he considered "the only town [he] ever saw that has been built at all in accordance with the advanced science, taste, and enterprising spirit that are supposed to distinguish the nineteenth century." In 1964 there took place the first of four major exhibitions honoring Olmsted's many contributions to the American landscape—particularly its cities. It was co-sponsored by the Department of Landscape Architecture of Harvard University and the American Society of Landscape Architects. It is not accidental, I think, that this interest in Olmsted should have accompanied a rising painful awareness of the neglect of America's urban centers. Olmsted was America's first environmental planner to comprehend the full import of the urbanization process for the future of civilization. In 1970, as part of the celebration of the centennial of the Metropolitan Museum of Art, an exhibition, "The Rise of an American Architecture," included an important section on public parks, emphasizing Olmsted's contributions to cities. And in 1972, in commemoration of Olmsted's one-hundred-and-fiftieth birthday, there took place two major exhibitions—in New York City and in Washington, D.C.—as well as local ones honoring his contributions to such cities as Buffalo and Atlanta.

All of these exhibitions, accompanied by various publications, marked a renewed interest in environmental planning and design most reminiscent of the nineteenth century. In addition, during this same period there has emerged a more vigorous profession of landscape architecture. In various publications and accomplished works, landscape architects such as Ian McHarg, Philip Lewis, Lawrence Halprin, and M. Paul Friedberg have provided new ways of studying the planning of open spaces. And at various academic centers throughout the land new curricula have been developed to train practitioners of landscape design to be more scientifically aware.

Optimism regarding the future of open-space planning in cities is also warranted because of the revitalization of sections of core cities that had declined very badly. These endeavors have been geared to historic restoration and preservation. To date, much of the emphasis has been placed on the individual houses involved— generally brownstones—which have unique architectural qualities. But the importance of the historic, planned open spaces of a given neighborhood is increasingly recognized. Brooklyn Heights, for example, is noted for its Esplanade, and Park Slope, also in Brooklyn, for its proximity to Olmsted and Vaux's Prospect Park, just as the renewed brownstone area of the West Side of Manhattan is tied to Central Park. Hence, throughout the country—in Minneapolis and Buffalo, for example— open spaces, even where the general area may have deteriorated, have tended to attract, at least on the surrounding streets, a stable and enlightened group of home-owners who understand the importance of the space and are prepared to fight for its maintenance and improvement. This movement toward historic recognition of homes and the spaces to which they are tied physically and functionally has not yet peaked and contributes to a more meaning-ful discussion of the functions of all open spaces in urban areas.

Hence, Whitaker and Browne are essen-tially correct in noting a rise in expectation and some optimism regarding the place of public parks in American urban life dating from the 1960's. And PARKS FOR PEOPLE deserves careful reading by all who are interested in the improvement of urban open spaces. The authors have successfully translated the forms of more than a century of Anglo-American environmental tradition into the various processes by which much of the parkland in England and America was created. And they have applied these principles to the needs of everyman today. It is a considerable achievement.

ALBERT FEIN
Director of Urban Studies,
The Brooklyn Center,
Long Island University

June 25, 1973

xiv

Preface

In 1965 a successful revolution was launched in the parks of New York City. It was a peaceful coup, led with style and dynamic flair by Tom Hoving, who at the age of 35 had been put in charge of one of New York's major problems. As had happened in other cities, parks were ceasing to play any part in people's lives; visitors to Brooklyn's neglected Prospect Park had fallen by two-thirds in 15 years. Mugging and vandalism had made Central Park — once the world's cynosure — unsafe by day and lethal by night (Lenny Bruce used to say that the only women visible were police officers in disguise). Working from Jane Jacobs' belief that popular use of the parks is the best policeman, Hoving set out to show that it is possible to make them a centre for the lives of New Yorkers. Communities were consulted as to what they needed. A target was set of at least some form of park being provided for every eight blocks. Vacant building-lots were put to use with portable mini-parks and children's playgrounds. Rooftops in business and commercial districts were made into daytime oases for workers. Hoving banned all cars from Central Park at weekends and hired out bicycles instead — with the result that crime fell and families from all segments of New York took to meeting there. Since 1965 the numbers using Central Park have been increasing by some ten per cent annually.

Together with his successor August Heckscher, 'Hip Hip' Hoving built new parks and sixty children's pools in the crowded slum areas. Design competitions were held; architects such as Marcel Breuer, Felix Candela and Philip Johnson produced new recreational structures, and work was started on restoring Central and Prospect Parks to their original plans. In 1967 for the first time the Metropolitan Opera gave free open-air performances in parks throughout the city. Poets gave readings without being — as they had been previously — prosecuted. Crowded costume parties, kite-flying competitions and fashion parades were held. Artists designed a Kinetic Environment, with a Rain Tree, a Smell Tree, a Bubble Machine, and an aluminium pond and a string of helium balloons. The Parks department provided chalks for contests in sidewalk pavement decoration; five thousand members of the public took advantage of an open invitation to come and paint on a canvas a hundred yards long.

The change in the parks had subtle effects on New Yorkers. They interrupted their apologies for their city, and almost began to take pride in it. Some people even started to talk to each other. No miracle occurred and New York did not become paradise. But a new dimension had been added to urban life.

To our children

Parks for People

1 The need for parks

'A City is not built wholly for the sake of Shelter, but ought to be so contrived, that besides more civil Conveniences there may be handsome space left for Squares, Courses for Chariots, Gardens, Places to take the Air in, for Swimming, and the like, both for Amusement and for Recreation.'
— L.B. Alberti (1484).

Why do people need parks? With so many other claims pressing on crowded cities, why should anything so uneconomic take up valuable space?

The feeling most people have for open countryside may be an inherited urge for the primaeval forests from which we primates come; our passions for gardening, allotments, country cottages and listening to 'The Archers' perhaps derive subconsciously from our ancestors' agricultural past. Those with little or no garden feel an instinctive need for greenery and spatial release. Such feelings run deep and can produce extraordinary results. During the siege of Leningrad, the inhabitants used their furniture and even the doors off their houses for fuel rather than cut down the city's trees. People, like every other organism, are affected by the environment in which they live. Lord Holford says that his objective would be to have at least one tree visible from every home (though a

recent 'plant-a-tree' poster campaign in San Francisco received a setback when the designer admitted that the highly-praised picture was in fact one of a marijuana bush). Orchards, such as are planned to encircle Brasilia, could transform most cities. But for many urban dwellers today the parks are their only chance of knowing the change of the seasons.

The need for public open space in cities is increasing, with the rises in longevity, mobility and leisure of the growing proportion of people who live in urban areas. 5,000 new people a week are moving to Rio de Janeiro. Ten years from now, Lima will have more than 3 million inhabitants, Bogota 5 million, Buenos Aires 9 million, Calcutta 15 million.

It is estimated that the population of the United States is going to double by the end of the century, while the demand for outdoor recreation in that period will at least treble. The density of people in Britain already reaches 790 per square mile; despite the picture the British have of themselves as country-lovers, more than 80% of the population are living in towns and 40% are concentrated in a mere seven conurbations. Her population is projected to rise by almost a further 20 million people — a thousand a day — by 2000 A.D. The number and the use of cars is likely to explode by multiplying several times. Are

future scenes like those in Godard's film 'Weekend' so imaginary?

A decent caution is advisable in predicting how people may be living in thirty years' time, but even now the large number of families who live in high flats have no garden in which to relax, and if high-rise building continues, it will be necessary for the ground-area saved to be used for public open space. Can it really be the right priority to give cars more space and expenditure than children in our town-planning? According to some biologists, human beings are beginning to exhibit the traits of aggression which species of animals show when they are overcrowded. (Peter Hall suggests the same is true about cars and their drivers.) Islands of lebensraum become all the more essential as modern living becomes increasingly complex, fast, noisy and crowded. Schopenhauer's theory was that people are like hedgehogs, uncomfortable and pricking each other when too closely packed, though miserable when isolated. In earlier times the countryside was close at hand; now that traffic-jams and urban sprawl make the sea and unspoilt country less easily accessible to the increasing numbers who live in cities, we must provide the living space and rural escape near to their homes.

Still eyes in the hurricane of the city, parks can provide safety valves for the tension of modern life: temporary additional territory for human animals when they are feeling penned in, to recuperate and regenerate, where people can emerge from the caves of their rooms to

3 Car parks - or grass, trees and playgrounds?
4 New York playground

8

complexity of trees gives mystery — boundaries concealed

park appears to run into infinity

large sheet of water joins sky to earth

5 Creating and extending space

stroll, sit or lie. The gift which parks can give is to be able to enlarge people's freedom in a limited space.

Villages used to have their green which also acted as the *agora.* But now that traffic has taken urban streets and squares away from the pedestrian (except in a few places like Dubrovnik which remind us of what we have lost), parks provide places where the value and scale of the individual can still be respected. Together with traffic-free precincts and piazzas they should not be isolated islands of refuge but should flow, linked, right through the busiest areas of activity. In Venice or Dubrovnik one hardly notices the absence of parks because one can walk at will, but only a very few other towns, mainly in Switzerland, approach the ideal of having parkways in which people can walk safely

Open space integrated with the urban scene

6 Open space integrated with the town
7 The need for parks: Runnymede on a sunny day

from their homes to work, shops and schools.

Pitt the elder used to describe the parks as the lungs of London. Urban green has practical uses as well as being breathing-space: it acts as a filter for noise, heat, fumes and smells. Each five yards' depth of trees absorbs and reduces noise by one decibel; and during the summer months greenery serves to cool cities whose buildings are storing and reflecting heat.

*   *   *   *   *

Before the end of this century the forecast is that not only the population of the world is likely to double to 7000 millions (and by A.D. 2046, double again to 14000 millions) but longevity and automation will mean that people in industrialised countries will have twice the amount of time for leisure that they have today. The length of the American working week is falling sharply: from 60 hours in 1925 it became an average of 40 in 1953; by 2000 A.D. it is projected to be four days of seven hours. In Britain the present basic working week of 45 hours is expected to have become 30 by the end of the century, while the number of retired people will by then have risen from 8 to 12 million. There is likely as well to be an increasing premium placed

upon the quality of leisure facilities, as education and living standards rise, while the nature of work changes from being physically exacting to being more repetitive and undemanding. But during the same period man will be 'finding a forest and making a desert' faster than ever before. Between now and the year 2000, in Britain some two million acres are expected to change from rural to urban use — approximately the same area as was taken in the whole of the period up to the beginning of this century, and a rate twice as fast as in the twentieth century so far. Very little time remains in which to save the remaining miles of unspoilt coast in Europe and the United States. If everyone in Britain went down to the sea at the same time, there would be about six inches of coast each. Every three years at present in Britain an area of agricultural land equivalent in size to the Isle of Wight is lost to developments of roads, industry, airports and buildings. In addition the advent of a new road, wirescape or tall building undermines the rural character of a wider area of

8 Derelict suburbs

surrounding country. And an increasing proportion of the open space that does remain is being closed to the majority of the population by being bought for private clubs and firms' sportsgrounds.

Although some cities such as Geneva, Sheffield, Washington or Rome are more fortunate in their environs than Birmingham, Sao Paulo or Rotterdam, the ease of access to unspoilt landscape diminishes each year, bringing increasing concern that the available areas are becoming overworn. Already plastic grass is having to be used in America. In Birmingham queues for a game of golf start at 6 a.m., but in the United States the line starts forming at some golf courses at 2.30 a.m. for the dawn tee-off. Some golfers have to wait nine hours; five hours is reported as par at one club near New York. Winthrop Rockefeller has stated that he foresees the day when visits to parks and historic places will have to be rationed. Exclusively private rights to beaches and sporting land are being extended at an alarming rate: the next generation of Americans may well face an unhappy prospect — if they get the urge to exercise, lie down until it passes off. The U.S. Outdoor Recreation Resources Review Commission, which initially began by concentrating on national country parks, was driven to the conclusion that it is the simple close-to-home activities which are most important to people, and that the urgent areas of need are in the cities and suburbs. But while private clubs are increasing in rich white suburbs, the city ghettoes which are growing poorer cannot

afford to improve or even maintain their parks.

What is a reasonable target figure for the amount of urban public open space? Abercrombie's County of London Plan in 1943 proposed a figure of seven acres for every 1000 people, which was modified to allow three of these acres to be counted in the green belt. But the green belt of a city the size of London is too distant for it to be of much use to most of her inhabitants, by comparison with the value for example the Vienna Woods have for a smaller city like Vienna. The green impression given by central London is misleading. At present in the old L.C.C. area of Inner London the ratio is only two and a half acres (one hectare) per 1000 people; Islington, Kensington and Chelsea, Southwark, Newham and Tower Hamlets all have less than 1.7 acres. Belfast has only 2 acres per 1000; Manchester and Glasgow are average, with 3.8 and 3.95 respectively; Leeds on the other hand has a splendid 9.1. At a ratio of 4 acres per 1000 inhabitants, London's open space deficiency at present amounts to 5500 acres, but only 656 acres of new open space were laid out in London between 1951-68, and in 1969 the G.L.C. planned to add only a further 28 new acres. It will therefore — even without the threats to diminish parks which are listed in a later chapter — be a long time before we reach the new Greater London Development Plan's target, which is to have a metropolitan park of 150 acres or more within 2 miles of every home, a district park of 50 acres or more within ¾ mile, and a local park of at least 5 acres within ¼ mile of each home. At the current rate of progress, Islington will have to wait more than 330 years for an adequate amount of open space; Tower Hamlets a mere 130 years. Amsterdam, despite Holland's acute scarcity of land, has shown what it is possible to do by increasing its area of public green space per head of the city's population from 2.2 square metres in 1930 to 10 in 1945 and 17 in 1965, with 28 proposed by 1975 — even without including the 900 hectares (2200 acres) of the famous Het Bos or Forest Park, the most ambitious new park made in modern times.

9 The National Parks in England are a long way from cities such as Birmingham and London

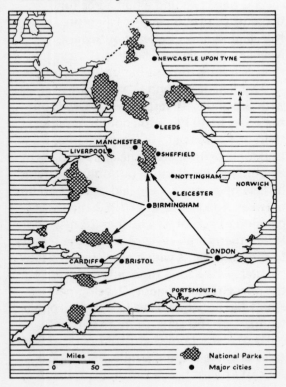

Miles
0   50

National Parks
Major cities

Prague, which already has five times as much green space per head of population as New York, plans 70 square metres per person.

In the new towns built in Britain since the war, the ratio of open space planned rises from 5.5 acres per 1000 people at Glenrothes, 5.6 at Hatfield, 7.0 at Harlow, 9.2 at Corby, 11.6 at Hemel Hempstead, 11.7 at Cumbernauld and 13.0 at Stevenage to 35.8 at Peterlee. But such a formula by itself is only a crude criterion: planning should be based on detailed study of the likely needs of the catchment area, including the distribution and location of the space (the distance in which mothers can push a pram for instance) which are the most important factors. Many parks are unused and particularly inaccessible for children because in the past they were built on sites which nobody else wanted; three-quarters of Birmingham's total public open space is concentrated in the south and south-west of the city. The value of a park is obviously greatly increased if it is close to areas of concentrated activity — whether shops, schools, offices, factories or housing estates — or if it is situated on a channel of human movement, like Washington D.C.'s Rock Creek Park. In London, St. James's Park's position is as priceless an asset as its design, and the 50 acres of Holland Park which the L.C.C. bought in 1952 are also particularly valuable because of being so near to the crowded shopping areas of Kensington High Street. Mid-town greenery is needed for office workers and shoppers which is within walking range during their lunch-breaks. In some residential districts

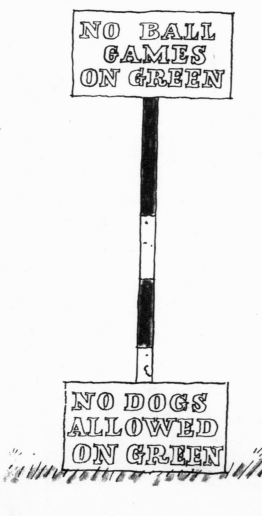

squares if they are open to the public can act as mini-parks. But in the heavily used areas between Mayfair and Whitechapel or in downtown Manhattan, Milan or Los Angeles, there is hardly a blade of public grass to be seen. Stepney and Shoreditch in particular are denuded, and Islington (where Pennethorne's plan for 170-acre Albert Park was turned down) is worst off of all, having only 0.47 of an acre of open space for each thousand of its inhabitants. 900 acres earmarked for public open space in Birmingham are still lying undeveloped through lack of finance. In Glasgow, where it is common for young children who live in flats above the sixth floor only to reach ground level once a week, it is estimated that a thousand toddlers' play areas and a hundred play parks for older children are needed: at the present rate of investment it will be at least fifty years before these are provided.

Furthermore, many parks which do exist lie wasted. Terence Gregory, Coventry's Architect and Planning Officer, points out: 'We all look with pride on the city parks that are visible from the main traffic routes. But are our social consciences as clear in the areas where amenity facilities are at a premium anyway? There are smaller parks or recreation grounds tucked away behind houses in blighted areas where nuisances occur, and which have been allowed to completely run down: long grass, play equipment which will not work, abandoned tennis courts, no flowers or shrubs.'

The demand for the use of open spaces is there. Ruth Glass's survey for the L.C.C.

found that an average of more than one visit to a park was made by adults each week: 81 per cent of children and the majority of adults had visited at least one open space in the month prior to being questioned — two out of five in the previous week. But rare is the council whose parks are not its lowest financial priority — the last item to be provided, and the first to be cut out or cut back. Nobody would argue that parks are as essential as housing or education. Yet they form one of the requirements that are increasingly essential for modern city living and which cannot be left to the free market law of supply and demand.

11 Salford, Lancashire. What will happen to the open spaces around the new tower blocks?

12 Parc Monceau, Paris

2 Some Brief History

Public open spaces played a very important part in the life of classical Greece, where groves were dedicated to gods and temples often had a garden attached. Xenophon brought back with him an admiration for the Persian kings' *pairidaeza* — pleasure-gardens of aromatic shrubs and blossoming fruit-trees from which we take our word 'paradise'. Julius Caesar's bequest to the public of his own gardens in Rome is the earliest recorded private endowment.

The word parc or park originally meant

an enclosure containing animals for the hunt. London's ten royal parks, like the big Paris ones, were once either part of the king's hunting forest or the grounds of royal palaces. Greenwich Park used to surround the Palace of Pleasaunce or Placentia.

Henry VIII hunted wild boar and bulls in Regent's Park and Hyde Park; Charles I enclosed Richmond Park as a hunting ground, of which it still carries an echo today with the deer in its bracken and spinneys. Hyde Park was opened to the public by the Stuarts, and occasional splendid entertainments took place there — from masques, firework displays, balloon ascents and the miniature naval battle which was fought on the Serpentine in 1814, to the Great Exhibition of 1851.

Most mediaeval towns had retained a strong agricultural basis; mindful of sieges, many of them contained fields, orchards and gardens within their walls. Vienna in 1480 is described as 'one vast delectable garden decked with the loveliest vineyards and orchards..... fishponds, hunting-grounds and bowers'. Over the centuries the influx of craftsmen, merchants and industrial workers into the cities led to an increase in population density. Those who were wealthy enough enclosed and developed estates around their mansions away from the city centre. The architecturally laid-out trees of the huge Renaissance park which Cardinal Scipione created for entertainment soon after 1600 at Villa Borghese in Rome, for example, was to influence Le Notre. Town houses of the rich gained fresh air by overlooking squares: the Place des Vosges,

in Paris, one of the earliest and still the most beautiful of all squares, was built in 1610, and Inigo Jones designed the original Covent Garden piazza in 1630.

The next century saw the 'English Style' of park landscape succeed the school of formal French design as many enclosures coincided with the romantics' pursuit of nature. The eighteenth-century designers would have abhorred the formal beds, lawns and railings of the modern municipal park. Though Pope described 'this scene of man' as 'a mighty maze of walks without a plan', most of Repton's theory of land-scape remains relevant today. But while Kent, Brown and Repton were creating private parks all over England for land-owners seeking mementoes of Virgil and Claude by which to remember the Grand Tour, the princes of Germany were making public gardens and 'people's parks' like the one which was opened at Munich in 1789. Josef II had already given the Prater to Vienna in 1776. Another imperial legacy is Dublin's 1752-acre Phoenix Park which, surrounded by its eight miles of stone wall, until recently had the claim of being the largest public park in Europe, and was originally intended by Ormonde to be a deer-park. Continental visitors to Britain however were surprised to find that the use of Regent's Park and the London squares was restricted to the surrounding houseowners. (St. Stephen's Green in Dublin, for example, was not open to the public until 1877).

It was not until Parliamentary Commit-tees in the 19th century began urging their sound Victorian (and economic) benefits to the health of working men that parks began to be built at public expense to help alleviate the effects of the Industrial Revolution. Kew Gardens, which had been begun in 1759, were taken over by the state in 1841. In design during this period the artist gradually gave way to the horticulturalist. The same era saw the dying away of the famous London pleasure gardens: Ranelagh, where Mozart had performed at the age of 8, lost its Rotunda in 1805; Vauxhall, where Pepys and Dr. Johnson used to go, shut in 1859; and Cremorne Gardens, which used to be able to hold 4000 dancers, closed in 1877.

The spread of building in the suburbs throughout the nineteenth and twentieth centuries, which restricted the access of town dwellers to the countryside, increased the demand for official action. The first Parliamentary Act in 1843 created Paxton's park at Birkenhead, which like Regent's Park was financed from the betterment of the houses which were developed on the surrounding land. Paxton went on to work at Kelvingrove (Glasgow), Dundee, and the

13 Cremorne Gardens, London, 1859 balloon ascent

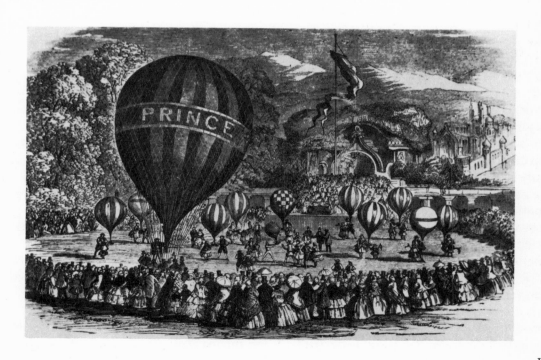

14 Paxton's Crystal Palace and Park in south London in 1854

People's Park at Halifax besides his famous designs at Crystal Palace. Sometimes parks were achieved by community action. On 13th January 1872 Hampstead Heath was finally saved from building development by a public committee (a fascinating plan to pump fresh air in pipes from the Heath to the City of London was however never carried out), and two years later the preservation of Epping Forest was secured.

The ideas spread abroad: *jardins anglais* sprang up across Europe, especially on the sites of former town fortifications, as at Cracow and Vienna. Napoleon III became very enthusiastic about such ideas during his period as a refugee in London, and on his return transformed Paris with the designs of Alphand and the organisational ability of Haussmann. In 1851 Paris had as municipal parks only the 47 acres of the Champs Elysees, the Place des Vosges, the Tuileries and the Luxembourg Gardens. Within 19 years these had grown to 4500 acres: to the west, the Bois de Boulogne was re-designed to vie with Hyde Park; the even larger Bois de Vincennes was planned for the east of Paris; the romantic Buttes-Chaumont park was created out of abandoned gypsum quarries for the north, and that of Monsouris for the south. 22

squares were laid out which — unlike London's — were maintained by the city and were open to all. By 1870 Paris had an acre of open public space for each 390 of her inhabitants, compared with only one per 5000 in 1850.

In the middle of the nineteenth century, the United States still lacked a proper park in any of its cities. New Yorkers had to use the parade ground at the Battery. Frederick Law Olmsted (the first man to coin the phrase 'landscape architecture'; Repton claimed to be the first to call himself a 'landscape gardener'), having seen Paxton's Birkenhead Park in 1850, started work on Central Park in New York eight years later. This, in addition to the unequalled strategic situation of its site, is the largest mid-urban park ever to made *de novo*. It is also, with its half-wild craggy outcrops and its constant surprise due to changes of level, as Nathan Silver the American architect points out, the best urban example of the English style of landscaping, because — unlike the historically acquired formerly royal parks of Europe — it was designed and laid out from scratch. The land it covered, which was then a shanty-town outside where the city ended at 42nd Street, was acquired as a result of a press campign waged by William C. Bryant with the help of Washington Irving and George Bancroft. Its cost was $7,839,727; the competition

15 Central Park, New York in 1863

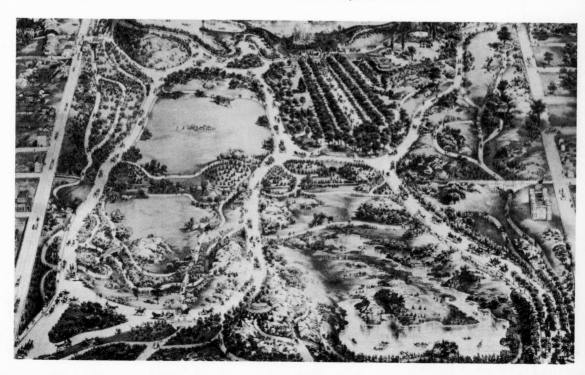

for its design with a prize of $2000 was won by the architects Olmsted and Calvert de Vaux. The plan was to create *rus in urbe* for the poorer New Yorkers, as Dr. Chadwick says, as a contrast to the monotony of their surrounding rectilinear streets. It still remains revolutionary in the skill with which Olmsted and Vaux — despite twice resigning in protest against political interference and attacks from the squatters who had lost their shanties — not only sank the through roads in cuttings (in advance of many parks today), but also used over- and under-passes to separate the pedestrians, horse riders, local and transversing traffic. Central Park was an immediate success both economically — it more than quadrupled the value of the property in its vicinity — and socially: it was visited by 4 million people in 1863, and by 11 millions eight years later even before it was officially opened in 1876.

Olmsted and Vaux made nearly fifty further parks in the United States, including Prospect Park in Brooklyn, the Golden Gate Park at San Francisco, Riverside at Chicago, Fairmount Park in Philadelphia, and Franklin Park as well as the original parkway system at Boston. Mainly under Robert Moses in the Depression, New York City's parks were increased from 14,827 acres in 1937 to 37,265 acres (including 9,268 acres of water area) today. This is now 17.3 per cent of its land, though only some 14,500 acres (roughly 7%) are in the City's immediate environment. Present plans include the turning of the 15,000 acres of Jamaica Bay into a nature reserve, and the development of the waterfront including the installation of floating swimming pools on the East and Hudson Rivers.

16 Central Park under-pass: the 1860s ahead of the 1970s.
17 The new Commonwealth Park, Canberra, designed by Sylvia Crowe

By the beginning of the twentieth century parks in Britain were in decline. It is Stockholm, Amsterdam, Canberra and several cities in Switzerland and Germany which have taken the lead in planning parkland as an integral part of the total

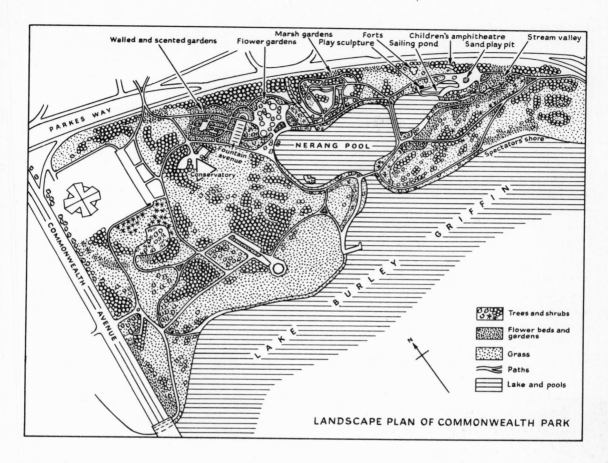

Walled and scented gardens Flower gardens Marsh gardens Forts Children's amphitheatre Stream valley
Play sculpture Sailing pond Sand play pit

PARKES WAY

NERANG POOL

Spectators shore

Fountain avenue

Conservatory

GRIFFIN

COMMONWEALTH AVENUE

LAKE BURLEY

N

Trees and shrubs

Flower beds and gardens

Grass

Paths

Lake and pools

LANDSCAPE PLAN OF COMMONWEALTH PARK

urban environment rather than applying it like a cosmetic to left-over scraps of land. Stockholm's parks and water system, Zurich's waterfront, Dusseldorf's management of the pedestrian/motor-car conflict all give lessons in what can be achieved. Except for Adelaide, Melbourne and Canberra, most Australian parks look like afterthoughts on uneconomic bits of land, whereas Stuttgart's new Central Park and water-gardens have a powerfully beneficial effect on the city because they run boldly right through its middle. Other cities however are being left behind: wealthy ones such as Los Angeles, Sydney and Melbourne are particularly short of open space, and even London despite the marvellous parks it has inherited (over 80 within seven miles of Piccadilly) is in danger of failing to keep pace. Almost everywhere in British cities, high buildings and new roads have been allowed to make lethal attacks without compensation in the way of new parkland. Canal-banks and riversides are still

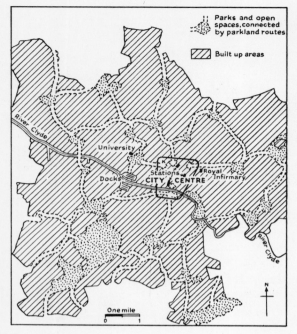

24 green wedges to bring the Green Belt into London have been ignored.*

The result of such failures in recent years all over the world is that the pedestrian — apart from in isolated islands — remains a prisoner in his own city. The inner areas of many cities, from Detroit to Washington to London, are now gradually emptying of population. This provides both the necessity for, and the possibility of, taking action to improve their environments.

18 Green tentacles: the trunk system of parks planned for Glasgow
19 Countryside in a city centre: section of the Glasgow Park trunk system

criminally wasted in a way that astonishes visitors from Paris or Amsterdam and even those who know Dublin and Sheffield. With one-sixth of the population and one-third of the rateable wealth of England and Wales, London should be able to provide the parks it needs, but the pattern is very uneven. At Clapham and Wandsworth for instance there are unattractive commons, left behind by the retreating countryside, unkempt and neglected. The East End and South Bank areas which have the worst housing conditions correspond with the parts which have minimal open space. For a quarter of a century there has been talk of traffic-free walks joining the parks, but even Abercrombie's 1943-4 proposals for

*He planned to join e.g. Kensington Gardens and Holland Park to Wormwood Scrubs and Greenford; Primrose Hill via Parkhill Road to Hampstead Heath and Mill Hill; Greenwich to Shooters Hill and Plumsted Marshes and also via Blackheath to Kidbrooke and Foots Cray; and Barnes Common to Putney Heath, Wimbledon Common, Richmond and Bushey Parks.

3 Use and Sociology: 'A feir feld ful of folk'

The concept of parkland as an integral part of city life first calls for knowing the way people like to use it — if it is to be socially alive and not just an arid planner's model like London's South Bank. A recent Amsterdam survey corroborates London's finding that seven out of ten people use parks when they are available, many of them regularly: 40 per cent of the visitors to Het Bos (the new forest park outside Amsterdam) go at least 15 times a year, and 52 per cent of the London park visitors interviewed in 1968 said they go there more than once a week. Eleven million people are estimated to have visited New York's Central Park in 1968 (the same figure as ninety-two years earlier). 50,000 people go to London's Regent's Park on a single fine Sunday; nearly twice as many use the Bos in Amsterdam. The recent Glass enquiry in London found that two-thirds of monthly visits are to the larger parks of more than fifty acres; and that 86 per cent of the visitors pursued passive activities such as sitting or walking, 6 per cent various sports, 3 per cent entertainments, while 12 per cent came for children's activities. In interviews it emerged that people considered the scenery and quietness the most important elements, especially in the larger parks; and also that half those interviewed wanted facilities for children.

The large majority of visitors arrive by foot, which suggests that parks could be made available to a much wider area of people if public transport services were planned to serve them — although there is always a danger, which must be guarded against, of development following in the wake. Bus routes connecting with radial services would be helpful around the perimeters of the largest parks. An enterprising survey carried out in 1968 in London's royal parks by boys from Daneford School found that a considerable number of people remain unaware of what, if any, catering and entertainment is available. There is no entry under 'Parks' or 'Royal Parks' in most British telephone directories to help people find out; and not many people know whether their nearest park is run by the Ministry of Public Buildings and Works, the County Council or their local borough council so that they can discover facts such as the opening hours or what facilities there are available for the children. In New York by contrast a special telephone number has been established and over a thousand people there each day ring 755-4100 for news of park events — an idea which should be copied in every city to help create the feeling that parks belong to the city's inhabitants and are there to play a part in their lives.

The attitude — welcoming or pedagogic —

21 Bureaucracy at work - parkscape with railings
22 The same path as it could be without railings

shown towards visitors will also strongly influence the use that people make of parks. Many of the more resistible ones still seem to be run for the benefit of bureaucratic by-laws rather than for human beings. Sir Patrick Abercrombie once recollected that when the Berlin police broke up a demonstration in the Tiergarten, the crowd who fled before the batons had been so disciplined by years of orderly conditioning that despite their panic they kept rigidly to the paths. Kew gains over the Pré Catalan in Paris in the freedom it allows people to walk on the grass; French parks have thick crops of 'PELOUSE INTERDITE' which makes them two-dimensional picture-postcard views instead of countryside to be enjoyed.

When Mr. R. Macmillan arrived as director of Manchester's parks, he removed all the 'Keep off the Grass' notices and was able to abolish many of the formal paths which had been troublesome to keep tended. But in too many other municipalities the puritan and institutional attitude survives, with spiked railings more appropriate to a disused mine-shaft, admonitory and prohibitory notices everywhere, playgrounds padlocked on Sundays, and keepers instructed to blow a whistle at the first sign of people enjoying themselves. During the heat-wave of 1970, a mother was sternly rebuked by an official in a Camden park for allowing her one year-old baby to take his clothes off. Civic pride often appears to be expressed in ratio to the municipal staff's

23 Parks are for people

ability to curb and regiment nature. Some parks are regarded as green and promised lands into which the public are only occasionally allowed on sufferance; their (devoted) staff seem to share the attitude of the keeper of the British Museum who once said that ideally he'd like to keep people out completely. In 1970 a London businessman was surprised to be fined £8 under a Victorian law which gives officials the right to eject anyone walking at any time in Hyde Park. Until people protested, nobody was allowed into Havant's Leigh Park except on weekend afternoons — and then they were charged entrance-fees. Even in post-revolutionary Prague, the public are permitted to visit the Royal park only on a few days in the year. In many a public park which was formerly part of a private estate, there remains a feeling that it still is private

property and the lower orders are un-welcome trespassers who should be under no illusion that they now own it. Gramercy park in New York is still exclusively for residents, and London squares which could be pocket handkerchief parks for the neigh-bourhood remain railed, padlocked, and empty save for poodle-dogs and an occasion-al nursery-maid in a starched apron — a sad regression from the life of the village greens which were their predecessors. Councils should be stimulated into acquiring them for public benefit: by making use of Repton's principle of 'apparent extent', a great deal can be made of a little area.

Some parks' gates are religiously pad-locked at 6 o'clock sharp summer and winter (whether or not the railings on either side still exist). Instead of a keeper ringing a bell as though it were a leper colony and shouting 'All out' an hour before sunset, parks should be lit and enjoyed in the evenings. In London, Russell Square (although its lighting is partly in an unfortunate emerald green) is among the very few to be floodlit. Those who have seen people tobogganing beneath the lights on Primrose Hill on winter nights will know the opportunities that are being missed in other places. Public tennis-courts should be floodlit for use if desired at night in the warmer months. Much more enterprising efforts could also be made to overcome the unpredictability of climate by means of sliding roofs, and outdoor heating for cafe tables and swimming pools.

Although the emphasis may now be passing from horticulture to recreation (a wide term, including some forms where it is

far from certain what it is that is being recreated), the sine qua non to remember is that the vast majority of people go to parks for peace and quiet. While developing the positive functions which a park can perform in a community, one should not lose sight of the fact that most users principally require well designed natural surroundings of grass, trees and water as a haven from the surrounding turmoil. With land and money limited, careful and skilled planning is essential to see that ranges of minority needs are provided without conflict between each other or destroying the whole.

The Glass analysis in 1966-8 found there were six main groups of park-users:

(i) mothers and small children, who want to be able to easily reach parks with sand- pits and play facilities;
(ii) 4-12 year olds, who like animals and birds, and want interesting play areas and plenty of room for active ball games;
(iii) teenagers, who are interested in swim- ming, sports and entertainments, and also like space to flop about in;
(iv) young adults, who want places to court, to take young families, to walk and to picnic or lie about on the grass;
(v) the middle-aged, who like parks where they can walk, sit and talk, especially at lunch-time near to where they work;
(vi) the elderly who, like group (i), want easily accessible near-by parks where they can sit and chat and watch younger people and their activities.

Obviously, parks have a valuable role to

Battersea Park
Lake hemmed in by "natural" vegetation — giving strong sense of enclosure

25 Parkland reclaimed from derelict land in the nineteenth century

26 An entertainment park need not be ugly: Tivoli, Copenhagen

play in alleviating the loneliness which is such a blight of city life, particularly for the two largest segments of frequently lonely people — the young and the elderly. These two groups are the ones which are going to make up the largest increased proportions of our population: in the next fifteen years, the over 65s will increase by twenty per cent and the 5—19 year olds by eighteen per cent, compared with an average rise of ten per cent in the population of Britain. Heated glass pavilions could provide meeting places for elderly people throughout the year where they could

watch the landscape and life of the park. At playgrounds solitary children can have a chance to form relationships. Mothers as well as children like an opportunity to meet at one o'clock children's clubs, since life in a tower-block is more socially idolated than in the old terraced streets. There are far more city dwellers than we imagine like the Londoner who said 'sometimes I could cry for someone to talk to': possibly, designated tables and chairs could be provided for people who wish to meet and chat with somebody else.

But when planning for the special needs

of groups such as the old, the blind and the mentally handicapped, it is important not to add to their isolation by creating ghettoes. Even well-intentioned ideas like scented gardens for the blind are resented by many blind people because they 'smack of segregation'. The greatest need of minorities is often to be able to participate in full society; the test of a successfully planned park is one where every type of person feels at home without resenting anybody else impinging on him or her. Urban villages are the ideal unit out of which to create a city, and each could have its equivalent of a village green. Clarence Stein at Radburn (New Jersey) — where it is hard to see the houses for the trees — aimed to make parks the backbones of the neighbour-

hoods. Members of the community can be linked in a common feeling of interest and possession by being asked to play a part in helping with the running of their park. One idea to encourage the people of a neighbourhood to involve themselves in the care of their environment is the 'trees matching' scheme, whereby a city or local authority offers some more trees free for each tree planted by the local residents. Children from housing estates and schools could each plant and adopt a tree which they then look after. There is a great fund of enterprise and leadership among ordinary people which generally lies wasted. All ages could be asked to volunteer with planting or tidying, and to form a rota of helpers at children's playgrounds who could release parents for work or shopping.

A well planned park should aim to keep families together by providing something for every generation. One of the most serious errors in some of the first British New Towns (and of many housing estates still being built today) was, despite the high proportion of children they contained, to erect all the houses before any recreational facilities such as parks had been provided. 20,000 people — the equivalent of a town the size of Stratford-on-Avon — are living in the Castle Vale estate, Birmingham, without any recreational area having been laid out. Open spaces are invaluable assets in town-planning because they are enjoyed by a wide spectrum of the population, and therefore form a unique catalyst for social mixing — ever since the days when Pepys used to lie and sleep in St. James's Park, and Charles II bathed in the lake there.

28 New York slum dwellers making their own miniature parks

27 Man-made play hill, Nuneaton, designed by Mary Mitchell

When Olmsted visited Birkenhead Park in 1850, he recorded that one of the facts which impressed him most was that 'all this magnificent pleasure-ground is entirely, unreservedly, and forever the people's own. The poorest British peasant is as free to enjoy it in all its parts as the British queen. More than that, the baker of Birkenhead has the pride of an owner in it.' Parks are theoretically for everyone. But for some more equally than others: often they contain an immaculately maintained bowling green used by a minority for a few hours a week in contrast with a derelict mud patch where all the children have to try to play.

Parks can become passionately loved social symbols. In July 1969 six respectable Hampshire citizens chose to go to prison rather than drop their protest about a proposal to put sixpence on the entrance fee to their local park. In April the same year several thousand people laid out a 'Peoples' Park' on empty sites in Berkeley (California) and in New York; shopkeepers gave plants, and statues and swings were set up before 'law and order' was reasserted by the police evicting everybody and destroying the parks.

The shortage of cheap beds for young tourists in many cities means that a small number of people sleep out in parks regularly at night in warm months. They include drinkers, one of whom described how parks can be divided into wine and cyder parks or meths and whisky ones, depending on whether water taps are provided. Railings, spiked or not, make no difference.

Incredibly, social problems have on occasions led to irrational attacks on the open spaces themselves: at one time the New York police requested that all shrubbery that might conceal anybody should be destroyed, and some vigilantes actually chopped down a beautiful section of trees in Queens Park on the grounds that it was a meeting place for homosexuals. Even in 1968 the G.L.C. planned to remove some shrubberies from St. Mary's Gardens, Commercial Road, because they had become popular with vagrants, and a Canadian visitor who recently inquired why a tractor was pulling down a bush in Battersea Park was amazed to be told that it was because there had been a rape behind it during the previous week! Co-operation in environmental planning between neighbours is traditionally almost always negative — a temporary unity to fight some developer's threat. But there is no reason why it should not be creative. Joint involvement in the running of open spaces can contribute with a sense of belonging and a sense of territory — to a feeling of community. Although it is the lower income groups with fewer private gardens and less chance of visiting the country who have the most urgent need of parks, open spaces can provide experience of community co-operation for all

types of neighbourhood. In the Ladbroke area of Kensington, common garden areas in the centre of blocks are run by neighbourhood committees. The local council collects a small extra rate for the cost of upkeep on behalf of the committee.

A survey carried out by Shankland, Cox in the new Wates estate at Croydon found that the (admittedly middle-class) residents were willing to pay £156 a year for good landscaping, and that they preferred to manage the shared open space themselves — which has the bonus effects of rapidly integrating newcomers and encouraging friendships on the estate (especially if there are separate places for children to play). Although the feeling for one's own patch of private soil runs deep (most of the Ladbroke houses also have a private patio) there are better opportunities for landscaping and large trees in Ladbroke-type schemes than in a medley of fences and individual patches.

By contrast and at the other extreme of social planning, parks and walkways being projected for Lansbury will be fenced off from the surrounding housing estate. This lamentable result of administrative division between housing and park departments not only unnecessarily restricts access but causes a net detrimental effect by creating a barrier between neighbouring homes. In all park planning, it is vital to integrate open spaces as readily accessible interlocking parts of the urban scene not segregated on the other side of a fence or a busy major road with entrances a mile apart. Parks need life as much as vice versa. They should be visualised as part of the city's fabric; not as

29 Arcadia Street! Open space in Lansbury, east London

something separate or turning its back, but
being planned inwards as part of the
neighbourhood's needs. The danger of Parks
Committees falling out of touch with — or
even, into hostility towards — the local life,
needs no underlining. It can be safeguarded
against by including on them locally elected
representatives of the catchment area's
community, or by electing from its neighbourhood a separate committee to look
after each park or open space.

Olmsted and also Sir Patrick Geddes (who
worked for the Carnegie Trust in Andrew
Carnegie's native Dunfermline) strongly
believed in parks fulfilling the needs of
the surrounding population. This tradition
is being revived in New York at present:
in areas where a new park is proposed,
meetings (260 of them in 1967) are held
with the local community where scale-
models and plans are discussed and
criticisms and suggestions of local needs
invited. The result is that the park will be
designed for the people who will actually
use it, and they in turn feel a proprietorial
interest in personally caring for it. This is
the best way to safeguard that Victorian
minds do not go on administering
nineteenth century parks when the
nineteenth century public has long since
gone.

4 Design

In an age of increasing standardization, the last thing we want is a standard park governed by rules and laid out according to some parks manual. Above all, urban parks provide the opportunity to escape from the oppression of bricks and mortar and there are an infinite number of ways in which the contrast can be achieved. There is a place for every kind of park and their variety is valuable — with parks differing from each other and each having its own particular character by which it is remembered. The basic requirements are for imagination and a sensitivity to the site and purpose of the park. The possibilities are endless and the design of parks could occupy several books in itself. Here, in limited space, there is only room to suggest a few of the main things to remember. To start this chapter, a series of illustrations linked by a commentary will best demonstrate the approach.

CONTRAST OF FORM

Parks don't have to be flat. By sculpting the ground, raising mounds, sinking valleys, the hard lines of the surrounding town can be modified, giving a satisfying contrast of curve against straight line.

Besides lending variety to the eye, grass pyramids and hills and curving lawned banks can serve the practical purpose of hiding and lessening the impact of traffic on the perimeter of the park, so that quiet sitting places can be created even in close proximity to roads.

The opportunities for thus shaping the ground occur everywhere yet all too often we have dead flat parks apparently thought out entirely in plan and left wide open to the impact of traffic. How much, for instance, the flat triangle of park at Shepherd's Bush, London which is harassed on all sides by traffic, would be improved if there was the protection of artificial mounds of this kind.

Shepherds Bush — as it could be

USE OF LEVELS

By careful use of levels a considerable number of different activities can go on at once, yet each be invisible from the other — in separate worlds.

woodland walk   tennis   fishing   boating   children's playground

Or change of levels may be used to achieve drama as at the Roche de Dom park at Avignon where ramps seem to lead up to the sky and the massed foliage of the park is kept until you reach the summit — a sudden oasis revealing marvellous vistas on every side.

lush green park ↘

views out ←

hard surfaces

Change of Level
& contrast of texture
(Avignon)

ILLUSION

In fact, this sense of illusion is one of the most important aspects of park design, calling for all the skill of the designer.

Far too many parks are merely patterns on a plan which when realized on the ground are deadly dull and can be taken in at a glance. A sense of magic and mystery is needed — the park must not reveal all its secrets at once or it will be a bore. Park design calls essentially for an ability to create and extend space. In some small parks a hill seen directly against the sky can successfully give an illusion of unrestricted grass and trees.

sky ↑

Primrose Hill

It is vital to conceal the real edge of the park by means of trees and groundfall, and to join the earth and sky by such means as reflections in water to give the impression of boundlessness which frees the mind. Nash's treatment of the lake in St. James's Park is an object lesson in illusion.

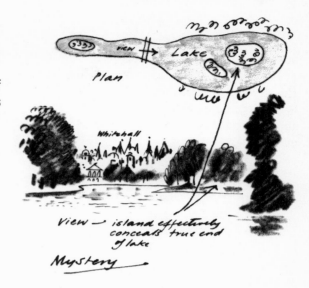

Plan

Whitehall

View — island effectively conceals true end of lake

Mystery

Here the flowing shape of the lake is interrupted visually by thickly planted islands which mask the true end of the lake from wherever you look. This gives a sense of mystery — the illusion that the water extends indefinitely. A cascade may serve both to conceal a boundary wall and also the noise of traffic beyond it.

cascade

noise of traffic muffled by cascade

wall

road

section

An important but neglected aspect of park design is the conscious control of what the visitor experiences as he enters and moves through the park. This calls for three

39

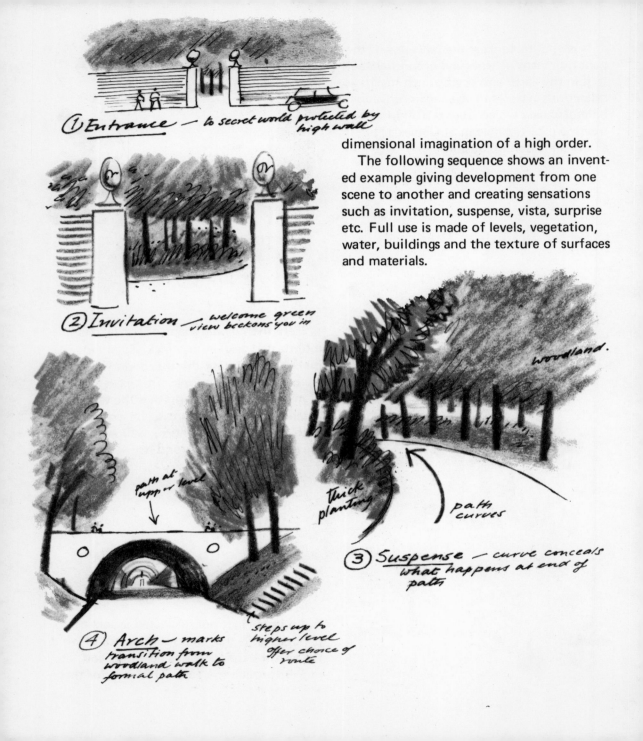

① Entrance — to secret world protected by high wall

② Invitation — welcome green view beckons you in

③ Suspense — curve conceals what happens at end of path

woodland.

thick planting

path curves

path at upper level

④ Arch — marks transition from woodland walk to formal path

steps up to higher level offer choice of route

dimensional imagination of a high order.

The following sequence shows an invented example giving development from one scene to another and creating sensations such as invitation, suspense, vista, surprise etc. Full use is made of levels, vegetation, water, buildings and the texture of surfaces and materials.

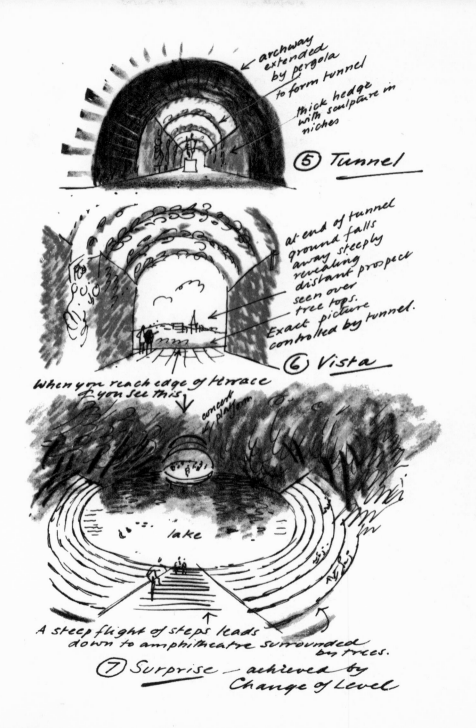

archway extended by pergola to form tunnel

thick hedge with sculpture in niches

⑤ Tunnel

at end of tunnel ground falls away steeply revealing distant prospect seen over tree tops.

Exact picture controlled by tunnel.

⑥ Vista

When you reach edge of terrace & you see this

concert platform

lake

A steep flight of steps leads down to amphitheatre surrounded by trees.

⑦ Surprise — achieved by Change of Level

PATHS

The handling of routes through the park
is important and sensitivity is required in
their design. For instance the mood
created by straight paths is one of getting
somewhere fast, generally the last thing you
want in a small park; while a winding path
through undulating landscape immediately
suggests a more leisurely contemplative
feeling in contrast to the directional
utilitarian pavements of the town outside.

gravel
path
winds
through undulating
landscape

TEXTURE

In parks which are intended for leisure and contemplation, details of design such as contrast of texture are especially important because there is the time to appreciate them. As it is, many new parks are split across by desolate tarmac strips like miniature runways. Yet an infinite variety of floor surfaces are available.

In the example below the main walking area is logically a line of paving slabs which will take heavy wear, while on each side a band of cobbles which is difficult to walk on deters people fromwalking on the grass edge and also assists the drainage. There is an interesting contrast in scale and texture both with each other and with the grass.

Of course the texture of the planting it-self is also important. This has endless possibilities in the contrast of rough with smooth, large with small and so on.

But there are dangers — of fussiness in particular, where too many different materials or plants are used merely as a gimmick and can give a fidgety appearance which is the last thing wanted in a park. The use of garish paving slabs in multi-colours also ruins many parks. Generally the colour of materials should be subdued especially where there are flowers, and attention given instead to such points as variation in the size of unit.

The contrast of path or steps against adjacent planting can often be used to give a satisfying interplay between rough and smooth.

contrast of texture
cobbles reduce scale of path &
deter people from walking on grass —
also act as drainage channels

43

CONTRAST IN GEOMETRY

Geometry is another important aspect of park design. Burle Marx's garden admirably demonstrates the visual attraction of flowing garden shapes contrasted with a severe rectilinear surrounding wall — an effect also seen in walled gardens elsewhere.

walled garden by Burle Marx
contrast of flowing garden
forms & rectilinear wall.

CONTRAST OF SCENE

The wall, like the mound, tree screen, arch or tunnel can be used by the designer to change from one scene to something quite different, thereby maintaining a sense of suspense.

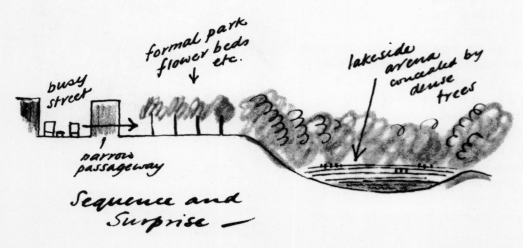

busy street

narrow passageway

formal park flower beds etc.

lakeside arena concealed by dense trees

Sequence and Surprise —

CONTRAST OF SIZE

It is also worth remembering in the design of parks that places of varying size must be provided: from the small intimate sitting places surrounded by planting, to the large open playing spaces, with all sizes and uses in between — and disposed so as to give the maximum variety. As it is, seats are all too often hopefully placed where they look all right on a plan but turn out in fact to be isolated in a wind-swept prairie or facing dreary views.

MOVEMENT AND SOUND

Movement is valuable as a relief from the static mass of adjacent buildings in small parks — not the sight of rushing traffic, but by contrast the soothing motion of leaves or rippling of water. Equally rustling trees and the splashing of a fountain can replace the harsh sounds of the town.

*   *   *   *   *

surrounding trees mask buildings

sitting alcoves protected by bushes

mound and foliage disguise boundary of park

sunken path reduces amount of path you see — also reduces wear on grass

small park in a heavily built up area.
no need for 'Keep Off the Grass' notices.

'In every other polite Art, there are certain established rules or general principles, to which the professor may appeal in support of his opinions; but in Landscape Gardening every one delivers his sentiments, or displays his taste, as whim or caprice may dictate ... Thus in poetry, in painting, and in architecture, false taste is propagated by the sanction given to mediocrity.' — Humphry Repton, 1805.

Taste in parks' design — whether a preference for nature wild or tamed, for floral clocks (descendants of the sixteenth-century Florentine parterres of scented herbs) or for Kenwood — may be subjective, perhaps for psychological reasons. But one essential rule is that there should be no division between function and design. 'The squalor of our surroundings' Sylvia Crowe rightly says 'is due to the habit of separating beauty from the other aspects of life and looking upon it as an ornament to be indulged in on special occasions, instead of as a necessary and all-pervading quality'. Television in particular with a daily 'counter attack' — type programme could help to change popular visual standards, in much the same way as radio and Promenade concerts have helped to remove the aura of caste from music. T.V. would be the ideal medium for regular short items showing examples of eyesores and improvements, which might keep local authorities on their toes with brickbats and bouquets and at the same time increase the public's interest in their surroundings. Notices in parks, to start with, need the equivalent of the revolution that the Worboys Committee brought to traffic-signs: they should be eliminated wherever possible and the remainder reduced to pictorial symbols and simple lettering.

Parks can often appear, and on occasions are, over-planned. 'Facilities for informal games' sends a slight shudder down the spine — unless it means just a piece of grass. Superintendents of parks are usually administrators, not specialists in design, though the two approaches and skills interlock more than is generally believed. Areas of grass which are worn and scarred or overflowing with litter are evidence which reveal a failure of design planning. Origin, destination, user and density studies are essential ingredients in landscape architecture; their neglect is soon revealed by the symptoms of worn grass turning into mud. Several authorities spend fortunes in repairing fences which are meant to keep people to paths, instead of realizing that it is the paths that are in the wrong place and should be moved to protect the grass. In planning to absorb as many people as inconspicuously as possible, a design should also take account of, for instance, the local microclimate; wind and sun are important factors in determining whether parts of parks or play-grounds will be used. It is equally important that a landscape architect is brought in from the start and not sought as a beautician later. Tree-planting for example should be an integral part of the design, not applied as a decoration afterwards. Isamu Noguchi says of his works and gardens: 'To me it's not decoration, I despise decoration. It's the creating of space, not the cluttering of space.' The importance of this approach is very rarely appreciated. Restraint can be as important as enthusiasm. The Esher report on York says 'The Corporation deserves credit not only for its charming floral decorations in St. Helen's Square, but for not attempting elaborate displays in the calmly romantic surroundings of Museum Gardens'; whereas Buchanan's report on Bath states 'The Parade Gardens suffer (to our taste at any rate) from a lack of skilled landscape design — a preoccupation with bedding plants and floral display is no substitute for real consideration of the functional needs and circumstances of each open area. The circle of grass in Orange Grove for example has fussy little conifers and flower beds which seem inadequate and out of scale with the surroundings. Beaufort Square has a patch of grass which is a pleasant foil to the buildings but is inaccessible.'

A successful plan for a park can take almost any form, provided it is not predictable and it is integrally functional, not 'beautified' — such as by using flowering shrubs (which can look excellent on the edge of a lake) to try to prettify commons or downs. Some people like their country wild, others cultivated; for a child, magic lies in one good sand-pit. Notable ones can be classically formal examples of architectural planting such as the Tuileries, Aranjuez or Hampton Court. Greenwich Park is at present being restored to the earlier plan of Le Nôtre, with a cascade of giant green steps which were never completed. (Le Nôtre never visited the site and allegedly failed to realise it was on a hill.) Massereene Park in Antrim, Northern Ireland, is gradually reverting to its 17th century character, and Central Park in New York is likewise being returned where it is still possible to its original nineteenth century appearance. But by contrast the original William Kent landscaping of Grosvenor Square in London was destroyed when over sixty fine trees were felled to comply with the Roosevelt Memorial design and it now has an uncomfortably close resemblance to one of the less elegiac municipal gardens.

Earthly paradises can be tiny and quietly intimate; or they can be apparent 'wildscape' as at Vienna's Prater, New York's

46 Wildscape in a city - riding in Richmond Park

Inwood Hill and Fort Tryon Parks or London's Hampstead Heath. 'Apparent' because such parks are generally not the result of trees and bushes growing haphazard, as Alexander Pope advocated in an article in the *Guardian* in 1713, but are carefully landscaped and tended (although there is no evidence for the myth that Henry Wise's trees in Blenheim Park reproduce the disposition of troops at the Battle). Designers of these revolutionary English parks sought unostentatiously to concentrate the pleasure and excitement of walking through the countryside, by planning and controlling a distillation of nature. But unless it forms part of a good classical layout, it is painful in some parks to see nature over-restricted with a fearful symmetry and tight inhibited designs with self-consciously regimented flower-beds, and trees crippled and mutilated from an unsympathetic lopping which passes for 'pruning'. Some administrations drive any sense of relaxation or rural escapism out of their parks by importing the disciplinary attitudes of municipal street-cleaning. It was said of the Paris parks at one time that 'the park police arrested falling leaves before they could reach the ground'. Some parks today feel too tidy for birds.

It is advisable when designing a park to make its plan flexible and capable of as much future change as possible. What is planned on today's research may become a Maginot Line tomorrow. In every country examples can be seen of parks designed for a former age which have failed to be adapted for changed needs and populations.

Nineteenth century society confidently made value statements about life and how it was to be best conducted. Many of the least pleasing municipal parks still suffer because they date from days of Victorian paternalism which are often to our eyes an ungifted period of design: fenced and gravelled paths between diamond-shaped begonia beds have limited attraction for most people today. As one British park official stated, 'some parks' staff are too busy bedding-out to think about readapting Victorian parks to the needs of the present day'. But the opportunities for achieving a rapid change today would be the envy of the designers of the past, when laying out a landscape was often a matter of faith and philanthropy for one's future successors. Mechanical handling can now accomplish in a week what would have taken the buckets and carts of Brown and Repton several years. Yet when we see the amount that the latter two alone achieved over a short span of years (sometimes moving whole villages in the process, so that their arrival with their sketch-books must have been ill-received by the villagers), it is clear that it is imagination and will which are lacking today.

On the whole, designs by artists have been surprisingly rarely used, apart from local folk-art variations of floral clocks and mottoes, or Gaudi's Parc Guell in Barcelona or the painter Burle Marx's cubist-influenced work in South America. The latter is one of the few designers to have attempted to match plants with modern architecture; his principal public designs can be seen in Caracas and Brasilia.

47 Waterlow Park, Highgate - trees and different levels
separate many different uses

Nowadays a competition is increasingly often held for the design of a new park. This gives a chance to new and unknown talent, although to enter can be expensive (Derek Lovejoy who recently won the competitions for the new Town Moor, Newcastle, and Everton parks, estimates that his entry cost £2,000 in each case). The composition of the judging committee can be the all-determining factor. There is a danger in all competitions which are judged by a committee that the designs will include too many items in order to satisfy all the committee's members. It is a great mistake to try to cram too many disparate uses in too small a space. London's Regent's Park suffers in this way, whereas Nottingham's Wollaton Park succeeds by specialising in doing a few items really well — preserving its basic design with lake; deer and camellia-house without adding any new

clutter, and by tucking an excellent adventure playground and golf course out of sight. Where there is no alternative to providing for many differing kinds of use, the best plan is to site the denser specialist areas on the access routes around the perimeter so that they act as filters, leaving the centre an unspoilt wilderness area accessible only on foot. This is the principle on which the United States National Parks are planned: Yellowstone, which has several million visitors a year has been so successful in canalising its traffic that beavers have returned to the park and are building within 100 yards of the main camp.

Waterlow Park in Highgate comes near to

being an exception to the rule against over-crowding: it just about gets away with four times as many items as its area can rightfully support, with the help of steep rises and falls in its ground. On a map its size is deceptively tiny, but like Dunfermline's Pittencrieff Park it is a good example of what can be done on a limited site by taking the maximum advantage of vertical planes — a trump card often forgotten. The roundness of hillocks contrasts pleasingly with the right-angled lines of townscape, and the rises and falls lend a park the essential surprise and mystery.

The horizon of London's Primrose Hill or Epsom's Nonsuch Park, for example, successfully creates an illusion of un-limited country in what are in fact heavily built-up areas; whereas a triangle of grass such as at Clapham Cross is visibly nothing which would be transformed by a small hill or at least some embankments which would shut out the traffic. The alternative solution of a saucer-like hollow, as at Fitzroy Square, loses through lack of privacy. Making a hill (shaped and contoured to suit its position) is the only remaining remedy when high building has encircled the perimeter. At West Berlin and Liverpool rock climbs have been made up one side of landscaped hills, whose slopes can also be used for waterfalls or skiing and slides for children. Some former quarries which could be made into parks contain peaks as dramatic as any in Arizona's lunar landscape. But in the age of the bulldozer, contours can be man-made anywhere: lakes and hills can be created, as Repton saw, by a single operation. Some striking 'landscape sculpture' of pyramid-shaped grass hills and water was created at Branitz Park in

48 Landscape sculpture

landscape sculpture

49 Landscape created from excavated soil - Guinness Factory, Park Royal, London. Designed by Geoffrey Jellicoe

Germany in 1855-63. A variant with a practical motive can be seen near the Guinness factory at Park Royal in West London. Soil from an underpass has been heaped into two mounds which conceal a depressing view of railway lines and by means of raising grass to the skyline hint at infinite greenery beyond.

In addition to a sense of identity and focal points relating them to their users, parks (as with women) gain from disguising their perimeter and not allowing their mystery to be fully penetrated at a glance. 'The extent of the premises has less influence than is generally imagined,' Humphry Repton said, 'as, however large or small it may be one of the fundamental principles of landscape gardening is to disguise the real boundary.' High buildings have the contrary effect and cause damage (besides intrusion) by delineating the finiteness of the limits. From some of the parks in Liverpool there is an illusion that they stretch unbroken to the Welsh hills on the horizon. A well planned park contains a varying sequence of intimate spaces and tempting vistas, so that the visitor is continually surprised and feels that he is experiencing a far greater range and area of country than he imagined the park to contain. Part of the subtle quality of many cathedral and university towns lies in the succession of hard and soft spaces enclosed by their architecture; in the same way several visits to a well planned landscape can each time provide unexpectedly fresh views, both inward- and outward-looking, knitted together with trees or hills.

Geoffrey Jellicoe describes his ideal as 'the creation and extension of space in the imagination. This is the main release from crowded streets. Three essentials are required: a sufficient complexity of trees to create mystery and conceal boundaries; a sense that the park runs into the sky in all directions; and a sheet of water of sufficient size to join this sky to earth. 'Walls can enclose a sense of intimacy, and also shut out the sight of traffic, but the sweep and freedom of a park are helped if barriers and fences are otherwise kept to a minimum — even where railings are as fine as those at the Parc de Monceau. Water or 'ha-ha' ditches are the best boundaries; cattle-grids are less conspicuous than gates; and where a fence is necessary, it can be sunk from sight — as at Runnymede — in a ditch. The south-east part of Hyde Park, by comparison, is blighted with chest-high railings, and if the Serpentine and the Regent's Park lake do not require any rails, why need there be a fiddly one round the lake in St. James's Park? Paris parks specialise in, besides ankle-height trip-wires, a particular kind of rustic concrete imitation of wood-fencing. Modern zoos, like the one at Basle in Switzerland, also show the improvement when bars are replaced by 'open-plan' ditches. Cages in zoos are no longer thought necessary to emphasise the distinctiveness of the human onlookers; they cannot be needed to contain the wild nature of parks from threatening our streets.

A good example of an improvement that could be achieved in this way is behind the Albert Memorial in London's equivalent of Central Park. The boundary between Hyde Park and Kensington Gardens (beloved of nannies and spies for assignations) was formerly a sunken fence or ha-ha, but unfortunately this was later filled in and replaced by railings. It is not clear why such a boundary is necessary at all, but the removal of the railings would both save the expense of regular paintings and — if the through road were sunk in a cutting, or better still diverted — provide a sweep of park unbroken from Kensington to Mayfair. The abrupt shock of the sight of country-side at the foot of the streets running on to Hampstead Heath would be ruined if there were dividing railings. Strong contrasts are the savour of city life; the sudden sight of

a fox adds an ingredient to townscape that no planner can provide. It is encouraging that the new open spaces planned for Andover will be unfenced. Manchester spends £10,000 a year painting and repairing fences, many of which are unnecessary. Wartime had a liberating effect on parks and squares, when most of the uglier iron railings were removed for scrap.

Unfortunately the Ministry of Works has recently spent over £50,000 in restoring railings round Hyde Park. Yet as long ago as August 2nd 1858 Lord Palmerston said in Parliament that he would like to know 'when it was the intention of the Chief Commissioner of Works to remove those abominable iron hurdles which now dis-figured the parks, and prevented the people of the metropolis from the free enjoyment of them, although they were maintained at the public expense simply for the public recreation.' He said that the late Chief Commissioner had assured him that they would be removed last spring, but there they were still, and there they appeared likely 'o remain, so far as he could see, until the iron had disappeared by the process of time. Meanwhile the public were pre-cluded from 'that power of free expatiation over their own parks which is essential to their health and amusement.' Perhaps Lord John Manners would say that the object of those hurdles is to prevent the people from walking over the grass; but he (Viscount Palmerston) did not know for what purpose the grass was there, except to be walked upon. If it were to be kept for the purpose of being looked at only, it ceased to have the advantage it was intended to confer upon the population. He wished to know, therefore, 'when the noble Lord intended taking the people of the metropolis out of irons, so far as related to the parks.'

Railings are in any event of only minimal use in dealing with what is perhaps the major problem in the design of modern public parks: the reconciliation, while absorbing the greatest number of people, of diverse activities without intrusion on each other. Central Park in New York uses its terrain to separate a series of different areas, some sweepingly wide, some intimately closed. Eaters, swimmers, sleepers, swingers, sportsmen, sunbathers, strollers, skaters, audiences for plays and music — all need to be catered for and fitted in, without turning the result into a chaotically competing jumble. Children's

play-grounds if they are a success are probably messy and — as proof of pleasure — noisy. Also, as Tony Southard the landscape architect says: 'There is a tendency to add recreational elements piecemeal to parks, like ice-cream stands, trinket shops and hotels gathering round a beauty spot until the original quality slowly becomes engulfed in things which essentially belong to the city street. Large parks should have a peripheral 'high-street' where all the busy functions and buildings could be gathered, thus leaving the bulk of the park in quiet where one could be capable of solitude.'

A great deal can be reconciled in even a small space with careful planning and by using grass banks, hedging, trees and water — both splashing and as hazards — together with variations of level. The Alhambra in Spain cunningly interlocks many different gardens among its buildings without seeming crowded; Holland Park in London

50 Village green atmosphere in London: Holland Park

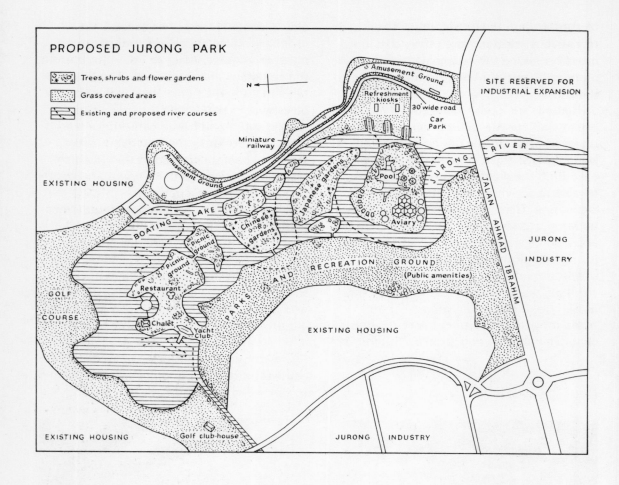

PROPOSED JURONG PARK

Trees, shrubs and flower gardens

Grass covered areas

Existing and proposed river courses

N

Amusement Ground

SITE RESERVED FOR INDUSTRIAL EXPANSION

Refreshment kiosks

30' wide road

Car Park

Miniature railway

EXISTING HOUSING

Amusement Ground

Japanese gardens

Pool

JURONG RIVER

JALAN AHMAD IBRAHIM

JURONG INDUSTRY

BOATING LAKE

Chinese gardens

Aviary

Picnic ground

Picnic ground

PARKS AND RECREATION GROUND
(Public amenities)

GOLF COURSE

Restaurant

Chalet

Yacht Club

EXISTING HOUSING

EXISTING HOUSING

Golf club-house

JURONG INDUSTRY

combines formal gardens, woods for walking, stages for plays and concerts, and a
playing field framed with trees like a
village green. The Jardin du Luxembourg
segregates its various compartments with
marvellous walls of horse-chestnuts. The
ideal is to have separate parks for different
moods and any activities which may
conflict; but where this is not possible, the
most effective insulations are trees and

51 An imaginative new park - Singapore
52 Het Bos, Amsterdam

water. At Jurong Park, which is being built
in a new city to the west of Singapore,
there is the ingenious solution of setting the
restaurant and picnic grounds, the aviary,
and the Chinese and Japanese gardens each
on an island separated by water. In the Bos

54

of Amsterdam, a fantastic range of recreational elements are embedded in an overall forest: 2,200 acres of polder were planted with several million trees, interspersed with canals and pools; a large artificial hill has been raised from the excavations of the canals, with a restaurant on its summit and its slopes used for skiing and tobogganing. The whole park, besides providing a regatta course, swimming pools, tennis courts, an open-air theatre, quiet places and nature reserves, is laced with separate systems of paths, cycling tracks, and bridle paths. At present the trees which absorb all these activities have a somewhat regimented feeling due to their grid pattern of planting, but with natural growth and regeneration one hopes they will gradually lose some of this formality.

Trees are a neglected solution for a wide range of environmental problems. They could be used much more than they are at present to screen cemeteries and crematoria, refuse tips, sewage farms, railways and sidings. The sight of an occasional orchard would be an implosion in urban landscapes.

Playing fields in particular could be improved by planting trees and shrubs around the edge (taking care not to let the branches over-hang the pitches). A wind-swept piazza such as London's South Bank could also be transformed by planting many more semi-mature trees — which in that particular instance would also do something to lessen the visual shock of the Shell Building. There is no reason either why the range of trees seen in the average park should not be much more imaginative: why shouldn't we plant more catalpas (which are so impressive in Budapest), tulip trees, pagoda trees, judas trees, scented limes, paulownias, trees-of-heaven or honey-locust trees?

Nor need they be a labour of love only for the benefit of future generations. Moving and replanting semi-mature trees is not new. Pliny, Seneca and Anatolius were among those who described it in classical times. Le Nôtre performed extraordinary tree-moving feats at Versailles for Louis XIV. In England under the Stuarts, John Evelyn records that he successfully transplanted elms as big as his waist. Lord Fitzharding, the Treasurer to Charles II, initiated the practice — later much used by Capability Brown — of pruning the roots of trees a year or more before moving them. Alphand moved trees up to sixty feet high in redesigning the Bois de Boulogne. In recent times, the National Coal Board has

53 Residential islands close to city converted into parkland with marina, Toronto

reduced the costs of the operation by developing a hydraulic transporter comprising a tractor with a large curved blade that can cut out a tree together with its root-ball. By 1965 it was estimated that the number of semi-mature trees being transplanted in Britain had risen to about 2,000 a year, compared to only 80 in 1960. Many of the trees were over forty feet high, and species which have been successfully moved include ash, blue spruce, beech and copper beech, birch, cedar, cherry, elm, hornbeam, horse chestnut, lilac, lime, Norway maple, oak, pine, poplar, rowan, sycamore, Turkey oak and willow. Sometimes the cost of moving and replanting trees is no greater than would have been involved in destroying them in their old sites. The Civic Trust has planted over 650 mature trees up to forty-five feet high in London, and has achieved the remarkable success rate of ninety-seven per cent survival.

After trees, water is the landscaper's next most effective asset — though it can become a liability if it is allowed to become stagnant. Clear water running over stones instead of mud can be very attractive. Paris' St. Cloud, the Generalife, the Villa Lante and Leningrad's Hermitage treat water in the grand classical manner. By contrast a tiny 'oasis' park in central Manhattan designed by Robert Zion, whose area (the site of a former night-club) is in fact only 42 by 100 feet achieves surprising insulation from the surrounding traffic-rush with the help of a 20 foot high waterfall which stretches right across the width of one wall. Anyone who has visited Rome or Augsburg will agree that British and American parks and squares have far too few fountains and that those we do have could be much more beautiful — though a pair of new ones in the lake in London's St. James's Park have recently been able to get past the Treasury on the grounds that they aerate the water.

The effect of Clean Air legislation has increased the pleasure of using city parks by removing the film of grime which used to cover their grass, leaves and water in Britain. For a cost of three shillings a head, Central London's December sunshine has been increased by 70 per cent. By 1968 the smoke concentration in London (55 microgrammes per cubic metre) was down by two-thirds of the figure when the Act was passed twelve years earlier. The sulphur dioxide content was reduced by 40 per cent of the 1956 amount though it is worth remembering that this still totals some 1000 tons emitted each day in London. New York however still suffers a daily deposit of no less than 3200 tons of sulphur dioxide, 280 tons of dirt and 4200 tons of carbon monoxide; and less than a quarter of urban areas in the north of England are as yet covered by the Clean Air orders, compared with 70 per cent in London. Sweden, where the onus is, as it should be, on an industrialist to prove that his plant will not contaminate the environment, has proposed an international set of standards for air and water purity.

*   *   *   *   *

Attention to the detail of design can make or mar its entire impression. This applied especially to the possibilities of

57

flood-lighting, at which Paris and, above all, Rome excel: the latter's use of reflected light is masterly. In Avignon's park, bamboo thickets have been skilfully lit with concealed internal lights. London's parks have possibilities for imaginative lighting which could transform them at night: an overdue start will now be made with St. James's Park.

Textures, as well, are all-important. Popular but visually undistinguished areas like New York's Washington Square or London's Sloane and Leicester Squares could benefit from patterned floors as well designed as those in Seville or some places in Scandinavia and Japan. Designs of setts or cobbles can take the toughest wear. Although a poor pattern can be disruptive, the floor of an urban space is as visually important as its surround. Inside parks, there is much to be said for trying to stick as closely as possible to natural materials:

the stone slabs of the winding path around the shore of the lake at Zurich are vastly preferable to the asphalt-and-rail of the traditional paths in most European parks. Perhaps at least loveable of all are infusions of what Peter Shepheard has called 'Godwottery': limestone-walls or Hispanoesque wrought iron straying far from the Cotswolds or Spain.

It should also be remembered that the absence of steps and kerbs can make all the difference to the use which disabled people are able to make of a park: this dimension of a park — its use — is more important than any dimension of its appearance, though each affect each other. Perhaps a notice might be pinned over each designer's and administrator's desk, reminding them that planning is the servant of people's enjoyment and should never appear to supersede it.

5 'Danger, Men at Work': Losses and Threats to Parks.

Parkland may be spoiled either by default or through falling victim to several kinds of attack. Open spaces can be eroded by misuse and wear and tear because of overcrowding, or from neglect due to bad location or design. Over-enthusiasm can be almost as dangerous as negligence: a great design can be gradually sapped over the years — as at St. James's Park where Nash's romantic vistas have been undermined by small fences, dinky trees and fussy little flowerbeds.

The occasional loss would sometimes be tolerable if it were made good elsewhere, but today in countries with mixed economies there is a vacuum in imaginative landscaping on the grand scale. A new layout is almost invariably a utilitarian adjunct of some building development, rather than being conceived in its own right as an addition to the heritage of our landscape. Where are today's equivalents of Kenwood and Stourhead? Where are the avenues of pleached limes or elms being planted for our successors? Private companies are not interested, and councils are too cost-conscious to plan the equivalent of the parks created by the wealthy private landowners of the past: afraid of being accused of profligacy with ratepayers' money, they feel that now is never the right time to spend heavily on items so conspicuously visible and pleasure-giving. There were protests when Liverpool Corporation spent £43,000 on the priceless 94 acres of Calderstones Park. One wealthy council in Surrey at the present time devotes £12,000 a year to tree-pruning compared with less than £1,000 on new planting, with a result that one inhabitant says reminds him of Ypres in 1917. Whereas in the United States there are some twenty-five university schools of landscape architecture, the country that was once the home of Kent, Brown, Repton and Paxton has only one degree course, recently started at Sheffield. Anybody who has had the chance to compare the landscaping of, for example, the southern part of the M1 motorway in Britain with that of the Merritt Parkway in New England will have realised the inevitable result.

Perhaps the most serious danger at present is that several thousand acres of common land all over Britain which were not registered under the 1965 Commons Registration Act may be lost as public open space. Parks are continuously vulnerable to many guises of attack and enroachment. Tel-Aviv for example (which

54 Miniature park in built-up Manhattan. The waterfall helps to screen traffic noise. Paley Park, designed by Robert L. Zion

55 Man and his car park. Long Island, New York

has all too little parkland) sold some off to hotels. Birmingham has recently decided to build on 1540 acres of its proposed green belt, and Tokyo in 1965 abandoned its plans for a green belt altogether. If all the proposals made for Central Park in the last fifty years — a speed-track, auditoria, restaurants, pavilions, a Cathedral for all Faiths, a replica of the World War I trenches at Verdun — had been executed, little that is green would now remain of its 846 acres, of which already some 300 are taken up by things other than grass, trees and rocks. There is now a proposal for a $6.5 million police complex to be built there, which would be twenty-three times the size of the famous Huntington Hartford Cafe plan and will steal another seven and a half acres.

Popular feeling about such threats need not necessarily be impotent. A widespread revolt by the citizens of San Francisco succeeded in defeating the proposal to run a freeway through the Golden Gate Park. In 1905 fifteen thousand people successfully defended Peckham's One Tree Hill from being seized and enclosed by a golf club. Hampstead Heath was saved from building speculation by a determined committee which campaigned for 41 years, but Union Square, Woburn Square and St. George's Square today are all under attack by different developments in London.

Danger rarely arrives now in so direct a form as it did during the 17th century Commonwealth when London's Hyde Park was sold off to speculators who charged entrance fees, or when Queen Caroline, the wife of George II, proposed to expropriate Kensington Gardens for the private use of the royal family. (When she turned her eye similarly upon St. James's Park she asked Sir Robert Walpole, the Prime Minister, what it would cost to do so. He replied 'Only a Crown, Madam'.) The most frequent form of threat nowadays is a 'reasonable' — in traffic terms — road-improvement scheme, whose line so often is engineered along the edge of some open space as the place of least resistance. Costings generally ignore intangible assets such as recreational values — which start at a disadvantage from being very difficult to quantify in monetary terms.

Although in fact it is often easier to re-develop obsolete buildings than to recreate carefully landscaped open space, the latter is defended by far fewer organised interests whom a developer has to fight. Developers in pursuit of profits and the wealthy roads lobby are two of the most powerful pressure groups in the country; whereas even if a public inquiry is held, those who use and enjoy open spaces lack the unity and often the funds to employ lawyers or a planner/architect to survey alternatives and put their case. Moreover whereas developers can set off such costs against tax, and the local council can ironically even use the ratepayers' own money to oppose their own objections, the local citizens — unlike suspected criminals — can get no legal aid.

The new motorway system planned for Glasgow will cut into no less than fourteen parks, and the expressways feeding this motorway will destroy parts of twenty-five major open spaces, including some which have many of the city's best trees on their perimeters. The impact that the northern approaches to the Clyde Tunnel have already made on the Victoria Park in Glasgow serves as a vivid warning. 27 per cent of the borough of Islington is already covered by tarmac. At Stevenage, a proposed new main road threatens the unique Fairlands Valley Park where a farm and a small stream have been preserved in the heart of the town.

If London's proposed new Ringway One Motorway Box is allowed, its route will affect Brockwell Park, St. George's Park, Tooting Bec Common, Mitcham and Barnes Commons, Hackney Marsh, Wormwood Scrubs and Wardle Park, even without allowing for any of its 'can of worms' interchanges. Ringway Two will affect another seven parks and eleven

56 Park Lane, London - as it might have been

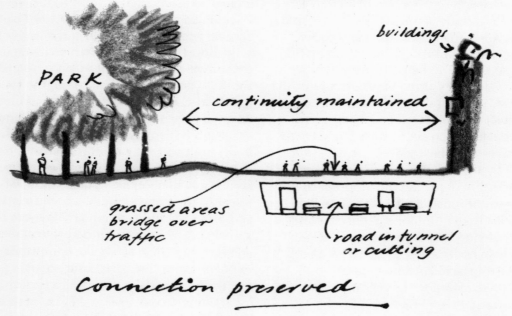

PARK

buildings

continuity maintained

grassed areas
bridge over
traffic

road in tunnel
or cutting

Connection preserved

In London, making Park Lane a dual-carriageway in 1958 swallowed up twenty-three acres of Hyde Park at one fell swoop; but prior to that a further 27 acres of the royal parks alone in London had been consumed by other road-widening schemes. The new Périphérique ringroad in Paris will destroy many trees in the Bois de Boulogne.

sportsgrounds and golf courses in south London. (Such are our values that the 'C Ring' road in one place has been allowed to destroy a public park in order to avoid a cemetery). Philadelphians, by contrast, are insisting that the Delaware Expressway be put underground and covered with a park. (Though it should be remembered that this can cause problems. Nora Sayre says that in Finley Park, New York, which runs over East River Drive, she heard taxi-drivers' oaths coming up through a bed of daffodils from the ventilators hidden there.)

A six-lane highway is threatened for Greenwich Park, which will run beside the Queen's House and cut off the museum buildings from the park. Modern roads have a totally new scale: the roundabouts planned for a new road through Bournemouth are each the area of three full-size football pitches. The new by-pass proposed for Esher will rob the common there of 50 acres as well as poleaxe it into two. Similar potential victims lie in almost every area, of which only the most famous — Christchurch Meadow at Oxford, the threat to the Cambridge Backs from the widening of Queen's Road, or that to Osterley Park from the South Wales Motorway — ever get known widely enough for their defenders to organise resistance. Although even the most philistine council rarely has the temerity to send a new road through the middle of a park, the commoner expedient of appropriating the edges does additional damage by creating a barrier which isolates them — as the building of railway lines did in the last century — from the city's life. The highways which girdle Manhattan similarly cut its inhabitants off from developing the amenity use of its riversides. The current alternative proposal to run a four-lane road in a tunnel under Hyde Park, although strongly preferable, can result in the loss of swathes of trees unless it is deeply sunk or is cut under a hill.

New buildings form a two-pronged threat, from the intrusion of their visual impact as well as from piecemeal physical encroachment on the ground. Administrative buildings which slip through the planning net have been allowed to permeate the park which Lord Bute left to Cardiff; perhaps the most eloquent example is Regent's Park in London. Although Nash's plans for a park-town of fifty-six villas together with a national Valhalla in the middle of the Inner Circle were never fulfilled, the spread of other buildings since then (few of which are architecturally distinguished) inside the south of the Park has made it virtually impossible ever to be out of sight of one. Despite fine individual items such as the Broad Walk and the former Botanical Society's gardens, the growth of Bedford College is in danger of turning the park back into an unplanned parody of Nash's original concept of a garden city. A huge gas-making plant at Coleshill in Birmingham's Green Belt is obsolete only seven years after being built. The most worrying feature is that when green areas are surrendered, they are never replaced: once land is lost nothing, other than a holocaust, will make it revert to park. Even temporary structures have a habit of becoming extremely difficult to remove: when the military were allowed to put a camp in Richmond Park in the Second World War, it was over twenty years after the end of the war before its wire and huts were removed and the area reopened to the public. A Finance Committee will find arguments to justify a new structure or road far more readily than it will grudgingly allow the cost of demolition. When a

temporary purpose has come to an end a
council will try to search out a new function
for the building. The result is that the
amount of greenery is continually shrinking.

57 Buildings and Parks - fantasy: Kew Gardens pagoda,
designed by Chambers 1760

*   *   *   *   *

The secret of a good design, in landscape
as in other things, often lies in its proportions. The size of twentieth-century building
dominates most of the landscape with
which it is in contact, and the scale and
congruity of buildings are never more
important than when considering the effect
they will have on the limited supply of

urban country. When Olmsted and Vaux
planned New York's Central Park, they
purposely planted natural objects to screen
visitors from the surrounding city — but they
have since been defeated by the rise in the
height of the peripheral buildings. Similarly
in London's Richmond Park; good as the
Roehampton flats are, their arrival diminished the scale of the park and destroyed
the feeling of countryside which the wild
state of its bracken and long grass had

58 Buildings and Parks - violation: Hyde Park

previously conjured. It was the 'human scale' of older cities such as Rome, San Francisco, London or Paris that provided their best quality as an environment in which to live. Occasionally buildings may make a positive contribution to an open space because they are of exceptionally good design (the Backs at Cambridge are a successful synthesis); or they can contribute a note of fantasy which blends with the escapism of open spaces, like Burges' castle at Cardiff or Whitehall Court's well-known silhouette towards St. James's Park and Chambers' pagoda at Kew. Mitchell Park, Milwaukee has three Fuller-type dome conservatories which are comparable at Kew. But many parks seem addicted to a particular style of prefabricated Tudor with a red tile roof for their sheds and buildings.

All too often a new slab near a park dwarfs the scale of the trees and is an inescapable reminder of where the illusion ends and of the ever-present city waiting outside. One of the saddest victims recently has been London's Hyde Park, whose initial rape by the Hilton Hotel (which after being turned down by both the L.C.C. and the Royal Fine Arts Commission was forced through as a dollar-earner by the Board of Trade) has recently been further compounded, even for those with their backs to the Hilton, by the towering 280 feet of the new Knightsbridge Barracks tower which has been built even closer to the edge of the park than the Hilton. Another 180-foot tower is now planned for the Woollands site opposite Albert Gate. Sefton Park, Liverpool, is also at present threatened by the encroachment of tall buildings of clumsy design though tower-blocks are now discredited on both density and social counts. Even if the last remaining large private open space in central London, the grounds of Buckingham Palace, should ever become a public park it would already be dwarfed by the office-towers which overlook it.

In several countries, areas that mas-querade nominally as open space or green belt are in fact only mockeries of those concepts because of neglect and the eye-sores such as heavy electric grid lines which have been allowed to criss-cross them. Wires and pylons that may be tolerable when care-fully landscaped they stride over the moors, extinguish any rural feeling when they are seen at close quarters in a more intimately scaled setting. Most of London's so-called green belt is of very low recreational or amenity value, compared for example with the forests surrounding Paris, Berlin or Vienna. The former is a classic demonstra-tion (the River Thames is a further example) of the faults of negative, as opposed to positive, planning. The sanctity is still theoretically inviolate, but nonetheless much of the landscape is gradually dis-integrating as countryside: trees are not replaced when they die, erosion is occurring in some places as more and more hedgerows are removed, and the detritus of luxury — old cars, washing machines, television and wireless sets — continue to be dumped far and wide despite the Civic Amenities Act.

The most pervasive threat of all comes from the ubiquity and increasing number of cars, with the problems they bring from noise, pollution and physical and visual dangers which have to be set against the liberating mobility and convenience of access that they afford to a wider area of population. M. Perrin of the French Ministère de l' Equipement has warned that the air in Paris now contains 92 litres of carbon monoxide per 100 cubic metres, not far below the safety level of 100 litres. In 1967 the director of the Bois de Boulogne ordered it to be closed at night to give the trees a rest from cars' exhaust. It is a system of great age and stability which we are now taxing with the immense amounts of carbon dioxide which we are adding from the fuel we burn. Vegetation is a great buffer: the forested wilderness removes a great deal of the carbon dioxide by the photosynthetic activity of the leaves, turns it into wood, and so sequesters it, giving out oxygen in exchange.

London's motor vehicles emit 22 tons of sulphur dioxide a day, although pollution from vehicles (of which the soot content and unburnt hydrocarbons of diesel fumes are worst) is so far only a serious menace in some cities of the United States, where legislative action has now been taken — a lead Britain has unfortunately not yet followed. In 1969 the Californian Senate passed an Act banning motor vehicles in six years' time, to prod the motor industry into developing a smog-free engine. American city-dwellers have been found to have minute asbestos fibres (which some authorities believe to be associated with cancer) in their lungs. Many of the most dangerous air pollutants are invisible. Car exhaust produces some 200,000 tons of oxides of nitrogen and several million tons of carbon monoxide each year in Britain, besides a lead content from petrol fumes which is finding its way into people's blood. Industry too is being shown to have unexpected effects on city life. An estimated 160 million tons of man-made pollutants are spewed into the air over the US each year, with an estimated 800 million tons over the rest of the world.

The minute dust particles attract water vapour which condenses on them and freezes, and clouds are formed which eventually dissolve in rain. The town of Belleville, in Illinois, which is 10 miles downwind from St. Louis, receives about 7 per cent more rain annually than upwind areas near this large industrial city. Cigarettes as well as smoke-pollution contribute to the 30,000 deaths from bronchitis in Britain each year; nonetheless its incidence varies directly with the cleanliness of the air, and is six times as prevalent in Salford as in Eastbourne. Britain's death rate from bronchitis is over fifteen times as high as countries whose air is less polluted; when one remembers that bronchitis kills almost four times as many

people as road accidents, and that pollution kills some 2,000 people a year in New York the case for large green areas in cities becomes cost-effectively convincing.

There are similar danger-signals in all the 'advanced' countries. In Venice in 1970, hundreds of dead fish were found floating in the canals and householders were alarmed to find that silver turned black overnight. Analysts attributed the cause to a deficiency of oxygen and excess of hydrogen sulphide. New York City's safety levels for sulphur dioxide were exceeded in the summer of 1970, and sufferers from respiratory and heart ailments were advised to stay indoors. Over 400 people had to be treated in Tokyo hospitals for eye and throat infections caused by a choking smog of oxidants produced by chemicals in vehicle exhaust gases. A hundred Tokyo streets were closed to weekend traffic as an emergency. The Greek Chamber of Technology has warned that Athens will have to be abandoned in 10 years unless radical measures are taken against air pollution. They report that the Acropolis will soon be invisible, covered by a cloud of industrial waste which is also damaging the marble. A forestry expert has advised the Greek government that lack of parks and vegetation in the capital makes Athens 'an unhealthy city.' Only 3 per cent of the Athens area is covered with vegetation, compared with 15 to 20 per cent in many cities.

*   *   *   *

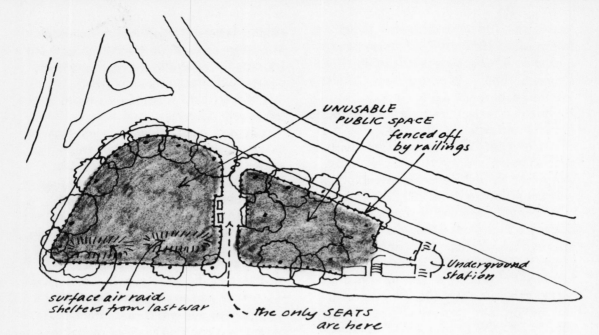

UNUSABLE
PUBLIC SPACE
fenced off
by railings

Underground
station

surface air raid
shelters from last war

the only SEATS
are here

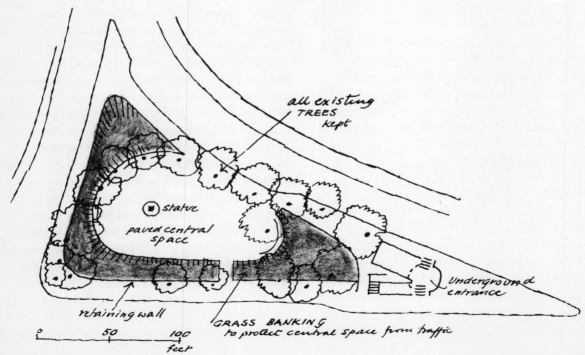

all existing
TREES
kept

statue

paved central
space

Underground
entrance

retaining wall

GRASS BANKING
to protect central space from traffic

0   50   100
          feet

One visually attractive way of blanketing the noise of outside traffic is with running water and fountains; another is by means of cuttings or grass banks. The roads inside and bordering cities' main parks should be sunk in cuttings or tunnels. Both the Bois de Boulogne and, in particular, the Bois de Vincennes are criss-crossed by a network of motor roads which should be thinned and sunk in cuttings because of the flat terrain. Long pedestrian subways under roads are no substitute: where there is a conflict, it is cars that should go underground, not people. In law, pedestrians theoretically have priority at all times in London's Royal Parks — but he is a rash walker who relies on this. Wherever it is at all possible the internal motor traffic of parks should be removed altogether. It injects tension and danger inimical to the relaxation of parks, and the accompanying street furniture of signals and notices is intrusive and ugly. The peace of the once-beautiful Villa Torlonia park at Frascati has been ruined by a wide highway complete with lamp standards. Lindsay and Hoving's decision to defy the New York cab-drivers and to exclude cars from Central Park at week-ends was an instant success; Rome's Piazza Navona is doubly beautiful with the traffic excluded — an island of calm in the eternally noisy city. In July 1970 Lindsay experimentally closed part of Fifth Avenue to traffic on Saturdays: picnickers, dancers, and miniature fairground trains — the only transport allowed — made happy carnivals. So far London has followed only with a limited experiment in The Mall at weekends. Richmond, Regent's, Greenwich and Windsor Parks are four examples which could and should be given back to walkers at weekends.

The safety contribution of traffic-free areas and open spaces is one of their social-cost benefits which councils sometimes ignore. 7,000 London children are killed or injured by traffic every year and the volume of road traffic is now increasing by 7 per cent annually. By contrast Stuttgart has re-built her bomb-damaged areas with traffic-free walks for pedestrians which are also well lit and used at night. Leicester has its 'New Walk' promenade; and Cologne, Rio de Janeiro and Norwich have made some main shopping-streets traffic-free, to the benefit of both the shops and the public. (28 out of 32 shops in London Street, Norwich report an increase in trade, in one case by 20 per cent). Besides the obvious effects on safety, busy vehicular roads can gravely divide and isolate communities. As Dr Chadwick argues, urban precincts should be as common as conventional parks. Cumbernauld has been planned from the start so that it is possible to walk everywhere in it whilst separated from traffic; as a result it can claim to be the safest town

59 An island in the traffic - now: Clapham Cross
60 Clapham Cross as Kenneth Browne suggests it could be

in Britain, with no road deaths in 1962-6 and injury figures that are only 23 per cent of the national average. Its Radburn/ Buchanan thinking has been followed in the segregated 'paseos' planned for the new town of Valencia in California. Precincts however should not be planned without regard to human reality: how many of them, which are well-peopled with strollers in the architects' drawing, end in real life by being deserted windy expanses? Nevertheless the benefits of traffic exclusion equally apply in many country parks: a survey carried out in 1964 in Cannock Forest among tourists (19 out of 20 of whom were motorists) found that 87 per cent preferred a trafficless area, and only 6 per cent opposed it.

61 Flowing paths connecting park to town in Stuttgart
62 Hyde Park or car park?

Cars bring more problems when they stop. Convenient public transport services for open space should be provided so as to reduce to a minimum the amount of ground which has to be relinquished to car parking. The open spaces of several cities have lost their character because their internal roads have been converted into parking-lots by commuters. Acres of asphalt have spoilt others — notably the old market in Gloucester; in front of St. Paul's Church,

Clapham; and the parking areas which (contrary to the original design, but at the caterers' insistence) form deserts round the elegant new restaurants in Hyde Park. The obvious solution, underground parking, is expensive, and has in several squares in San Francisco and at Cadogan Place in London led to the loss of fine trees; the trees of Madison Square Park in New York are similarly threatened by an underground car-park at present. The excavation can endanger trees by altering the water-level and exposing their roots. Car parks are therefore best sited under a playground, tennis courts, or roads which have to be bare anyway. The excavation of an underground car-park on the large scale of the one near Marble Arch was a badly missed opportunity to create an interesting hill on top or alongside. The saving of the cost of taking the 160,000 tons of clay away from Hyde Park to Heston would have paid for

all the cost of landscaping, and Geoffrey Jellicoe has prepared an excellent undulating design which would have provided a sheltered sunny amphitheatre and at the same time shut out the noise and distraction of Marble Arch. At other sites much greater use could be made of areas which are embanked and sunken, even if they cannot be covered, in order to disguise parked cars. Earth banks seven feet high are easily bulldozed and in addition help to blanket noise.

The best cheap camouflage is also the pleasantest: trees and shrubs, both as a peripheral screen and laced among the cars. There is a good example planted by the National Trust at Polesden Lacy in Surrey. Berlin in 1966 enacted a law making it compulsory to plant one tree for every four parking places. Screening need only be some fifteen feet high, and can be formed all the year round, by for instance, evergreen cotoneasters, eleagnus or viburnums (but not — because of their sticky debris — sycamores or limes). The same camouflage should be used at every caravan site (5000 new ones are being granted planning permission every year in Britain), scrap yard and rubbish tip in the country, and local authorities should make the planting of semi-mature trees a precondition for planning permission. Trees have an additional hot-weather advantage in a car park in that their shade keeps the cars cool, so that their owners don't return to tin furnaces. Weeping beech or willow trees can make excellent and beautiful bicycle ˙ds. At many places, parking for a much larger number of cars is required only on a few

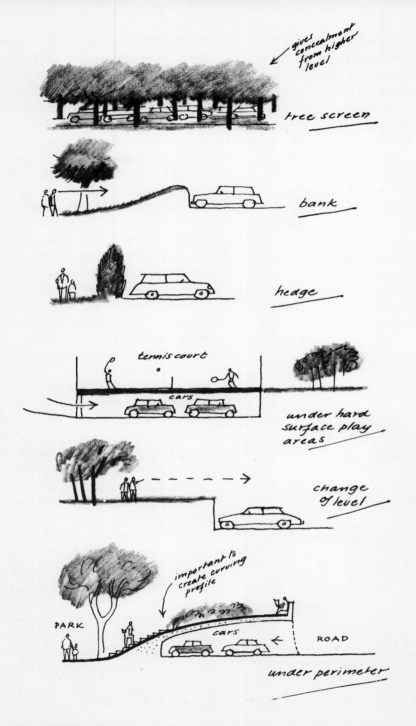

gives concealment from higher level

tree screen

bank

hedge

tennis court

cars

under hard surface play areas

change of level

important to create curving profile

PARK

cars

ROAD

under perimeter

72

occasions annually such as bank holidays. Gordon Cullen has suggested ingenious hard-bed areas which can be flooded for ornamental pools or skating when they are not wanted for parking.

*　　*　　*　　*　　*

What can best be done to protect parks overall from the various threats that hang over them? The formation of a vigilant local committee for each open space could provide a guard to watch its interests. This should not follow the National Parks' committees' error of being dominated by local councillors: on occasions it should be able to fight its council's plans freely. But equally, it should be elected by the surrounding neighbourhood to ensure that it represents the whole community and not just those whose houses border the park. If any loss is really inescapable, the minimum compensation should be the provision at least of as good open space elsewhere, although even this is often a poor exchange: the destruction of a Hyde Park for example cannot be repaired by the sop of fragmented scraps of ground elsewhere. Legislation to make compensation in kind compulsory would be the proper safeguard.

64 Screened caravan sites in Holland

Having looked at the large-scale damage to parks caused by builders and road-makers, it is also important to consider how to minimise the depredations of the humbler individual vandal. Invariably described as senseless by magistrates and the indignant writers of letters to newspapers, vandalism can generally be discovered to have both a cause and a cure: much of it is therefore unnecessary, given the trouble of research and preventive planning. Neither is it a new product of 'modern life': even before the eponymous Vandals arrived in Rome, graffiti were being written on walls in Pompeii.

Each nationality has its speciality. The Japanese remove blossom from some of their parks with the thoroughness of locusts. The British seem to find deckchairs an irresistible challenge. Litter, if only a transient stigma, is increasing with the growth of packaging in what one sage has called 'the effluent society'. The volume of rubbish is doubling every 10 years. The explosive growth in the use of plastics for containers has meant that an increasing amount of litter is indestructible: unlike paper, polythene survives being rained on or thrown in lakes or streams. Plastic bottles and wrappers are expected to rise from 250,000 tons in 1970 in Britain to 1,250,000 million by 1980. Priority should be given by plastics manufacturers to research to deal with this problem. Scientists at Aston University, Birmingham are developing one possible answer: an additive which, by making polythene and polypropylene sensitive to the ultra-violet rays in sunlight, would reduce them to a harmless powder when they are left out in the open.

The Ministry of Works spends over £15,000 a year in removing litter from London's royal parks alone. On this subject, the head of Vienna's parks says 'An appeal, a polite request, perhaps with a touch of humour, is far more effective in deterring people from leaving litter about in public places than the grim word "forbidden" or quotations from bye-laws; and this should constantly be impressed upon park-keepers who are in direct and permanent contact with the public. Here too politeness and civility must be the order of the day'. It is interesting how often the warning notices themselves, as well as fences, are targets of vandalism. Brighton which has hardly any fences in its parks suffers only about £150 worth of damage a year from vandalism. Mr. J. Evison, its parks director, comments: 'Fences are an anachronism. They are also a challenge, and you can do much more damage hidden behind a fence. If a couple want to kiss and canoodle in the park at night, who am I to stop them?'

The number of prosecutions for the more

intentional acts of vandalism and offences in parks and open spaces in England and Wales is — contrary to the general criminal statistics — falling steeply:

	No. of persons proceeded against	No. of persons found guilty
1958	1625	1567
1959	1682	1538
1960	1317	1264
1961	2001	1954
1962	1679	1632
1963	1892	1847
1964	1451	1360
1965	942	914
1966	505	483
1967	356	308

(The figures are for offences against: the Inclosure Act 1857, section 12; Town Gardens Protection Act 1863, sections 4 and 5; Parks regulations Acts 1872 and 1926; Crown Lands Act 1936 and Regulations and Rules thereunder; Commons Act 1876, section 29 and Commons Act 1908, section 1; Law of Property Act 1925, section 193; Forestry Act 1967; for offences against byelaws made under section 15 of the Open Spaces Act 1906, and for offences in relation to parks, pleasure grounds, commons and any open spaces under local Acts, and under bye laws, regulations, or rules made under any public Act, local Act or Provisional order).

This steady drop in offences over recent years is partly due to an increasingly enlightened interest by the police in the prevention of crime. A senior London officer who specialised in crime prevention said that he remembered his boyhood days clearly enough to understand that too many prohibitory notices merely serve as a challenge. He thought it much better to have a good adventure playground in each park which could channel the energy and aggressive instincts of young people. The work of a good adventure playground does not stop with its boundaries: the play-leader is in contact with problem families and welfare agencies, and its effects can make a marked positive contribution to the neighbouring community. The average age of convicted vandals in New York is 12.9, compared with 14.5 years for other delinquents. It seems almost always to be a group offence, and in the case of many younger children to be a form of play. New York has recently taken to heart the gospel of Jane Jacobs that the more people are using a park, the safer it will be. The recent expansion of evening programmes in Central Park, together with improvements in its lighting, has resulted in there now being proportionately less crime in Central Park than in the streets of New York City.

Portable walkie-talkie sets for staff can help to deal with the serious offences. But intelligent planning and durable materials minimise the temptations and so help to reduce the incidence of vandalism. Plantings of semi-mature trees are less vulnerable than saplings. Manchester's Parks Department has embarked on a policy of gradually getting rid of all its isolated park buildings, and concentrating facilities instead in a single structure which can also include a flat for a caretaker who can keep an eye on it. Cardiff cured wear and tear from children sliding on its artificial ski-slope by providing an artificial toboggan-run nearby. Stockholm has made use of television programmes to help the public's relations with its parks. Schemes like those in the lower Swansea valley where schools plant and look after trees help to create a constructive attitude. F.G. Breman, the head of Amsterdam's Parks, considers that good maintenance is itself an antidote to vandalism, and that people's behaviour tends to reflect the standards of their surroundings. (But at the same time, the planning and tidiness must remain unobstrusive so that they do not grate on the relaxation which is the whole purpose of parks.) Stanley Cohen of Durham University, who has made a study of vandalism, wrote in *New Society* that there is a sort of coals-in-the-bath attitude among some local authorities which leads them to a belief that 'if you give them new things, they just destroy them', whereas in fact it is the badly maintained and dirty property which is most often felt to be fair game for destruction, in the same way as streets which are already dirty attract the most litter.

The Parks Department in Stockholm has recognised that where you can't change human nature, it's best to join it. It used to cost Stockholm £15,000 a year to clean away graffiti; now the Department itself has erected a 'wall-newspaper' — the 'Klotterplank' — a special wall which is

freshly repainted white each day and is regularly used by 700 people a week (including both policemen and protesters) as a literate form of Speakers' Corner. Certainly the provision of adequate facilities for children, which are discussed in the next section, is the best cure for vandalism. When Spitalfields held its first summer holiday project in 1968, the number of children appearing in court in August and September was cut by half. A District Attorney in Philadelphia found that juvenile delinquency dropped by half over a five-year period in a district where supervised playgrounds had been made available; and a study in a British city revealed that delinquency had decreased in the area surrounding a new adventure playground during the period when it was increasing elsewhere in the city.

Vandalism will perhaps never be completely eliminated but study of it together with intelligent anticipation can help to reduce it to a minimum. Whether or not Bertrand Russell was accurate when he stated that 'at least half the sins of mankind are caused by attempts to escape boredom', it is likely that the more interesting and satisfying we can make our parks (especially for young people) the less vandalism there will be.

7 Children: 'Regardless of their doom,
   the little victims play'

'Once upon a time', Terence Bendixson wrote in *The Guardian* 'children helped sow the corn and reap the harvest, they frolicked on the haywains, chased the chickens and joined the ranks of the gleaners. Their lives were part of the adult world. They played near their parents at work and helped with that work. Nowadays, only in places like the kitchen . . . . or when they can help their fathers wash the car at weekends, does this old integrated world live on. Most people work in factories and offices without the children ever knowing how it happens. What is needed, and what is beginning to emerge, is a popular movement to emancipate children, as women were emancipated before them, from their isolation and boredom.'

The earlier age for marriage is shortening the intervals between our generations. By the 1970s, no less than half the United States population is expected to be aged less than twenty-five. But in the central parts of cities, places where children used to play are vanishing as the inexorable search for new housing, road and office sites proceeds. 'Where once there were verges, old cemeteries, even vacant plots now there are only play 'decks' or other heavily organised concrete recreational jungles', says David Eversley who is now London's chief planner. Not all architects are like Erno Goldfinger, who went to live in one of the council flats he designed: the architects of some tower-blocks cannot have experienced the whirlwinds at their base where children are meant to play.

Lady Allen's survey *Two to Five in High Flats* showed that 72 per cent of children under five who live above the third storey of high blocks in London are only rarely able to play with other children of their own age because no safe play opportunities had been provided for them. Mothers in some urban areas are reluctant to let their children go outside the door for fear that they might be injured by cars or molested. Even in the 1960s sites earmarked for

66 Sterility

nursery schools were still being taken for car-parks; yet at the same time two out of five of the pedestrian road casualties in the London area were children, and the total continues to rise every year. The only justification for a fence in a park would be to stop children running into the street after balls; but with the number of mothers who wish to work on the increase, the streets are frequently the only place where children are able to play, especially in the summer holidays when many youth clubs are shut. In a number of cities some streets have been designated 'Play Streets', where traffic is forbidden to enter. W.D. Abernethy of the National Playing Fields Association says that all streets hold a great attraction for a child. They provide 'light, movement, colour, people, noise, adventure and above all, danger.' But their temptation for too many children ends by being a fatal one.

Yet play is a vital factor in a child's development. Through it a child learns about his environment and discovers the characteristics of objects and of other people and thus travels towards an understanding of himself. Today children are encouraged to express themselves more freely than in the past; but at the same time the urban environment has become increasingly

67 Imagination - Birmingham playground designed by Mary Mitchell

hostile to their play. This even applies to some parks. Paris's Jardin du Luxembourg is irritatingly antipathetic to children: they have to pay sixty centimes to enter the simplest playground, and can't run or lie in the grass; when the schools are shut on Thursdays there are hordes of frustrated children. Most administrators cannot disguise their dislike of children and the disorders they cause: many municipal playgrounds, innocent of items like climbable trees or soft mud which might lead to a claim on authority, have all the security and invitation of a prison yard.

At least one city in the Midlands still padlocks the swings in its parks on Sundays — the day on which they are most needed. Children in parts of Liverpool and at Bibury Primary School have to use a churchyard as their daily playground. In the whole of Britain there are still less than thirty adventure playgrounds, where children can do what they like with pieces of timber, canvas, ropes, old cars and sand. In effect, as William Whyte says, they play by constructing their own play facilities. This is an idea which was originally pioneered by the Danish landscape architect Professor Sorenson, who noticed that children preferred waste land to the play-grounds that he had painstakingly designed for them. He built the first one, with the help of children and their parents, in 1943 despite the war on a new housing estate at Copenhagen. The idea was brought to Britain by Lady Allen, who has remained the champion of their development since. Many of the council bureaucrats saw in their idea a kind of heresy, replacing tidiness by anarchy. The first ones in London were set

up by voluntary effort in the late 1940s;
the N.P.F.A. later backed two demonstration
sites, one in Liverpool and one in London
(the famous, but now built-over Lollard
Street); today probably the most well-
known and successful example in Britain
is one at Notting Hill.

Some people actually prefer children to
neatness. For others, the visual chaos of
adventure playgrounds may make it
advisable to shield them from view, as at
Copenhagen, behind six foot high earth
banks — not grim walls or fences. But as
Patrick Kinnersley wrote in *Help,* Sorenson's
idea 'probably represents the ideal as a piece
of planning and as a community development. The spirit of the adventure playground is similar to that of the playgroup —
letting the children get on with those
things they have to do. Again, the
supervision of an understanding adult
makes it all possible. In an adventure playground, children can build houses, have
bonfires, cook in the open, dig holes,
garden or just muck about with earth and
water, sand and clay.' Their success is a
salutary lesson when compared with the
trendy equipment which architects tag on
to a new building development, but which
often seems to stimulate children's
imaginations far less than the architects' —
with results that can be seen where children
obstinately refuse to play where planners

meant them to and instead go to vacant
sites or the streets where the action is.
Another common mistake is to lump
'children' generically together whatever
their age; there is as much difference between a three-year old and a twelve-year old
and their play requirements as there is
between Hiawatha and a Senior Wrangler.

Playparks specially designed for children
were developed principally in Sweden,
Denmark, Switzerland and the United
States. Stockholm today has 127. The
London County Council adopted them in
1959 for free play by children aged 5—16
(parents are not encouraged to enter the
playpark except in the case of handicapped
children); and itself, under Peggy Jay,
pioneered 'one o'clock clubs' for children
and play 'pens' in some parks where adults
are only allowed if they are accompanied
by a small child. A successful playground
can also have a great value in mixing
children from different social backgrounds.

Playgrounds of all kinds should be soft-
surfaced: it is inevitable that children are
going to fall down, but it should not be
inevitable that they fall on to tarmac or
cinders. The play area of Hamburg's
Planten und Blumen park is carpeted
entirely, not with painful asphalt or
concrete, but with clean sand. The upkeep
and equipment of this playground are
imaginatively financed from the rents for
grave sites in the city's cemetery. Planning
should not forget the winters: children do
not hibernate. The playpark at Karlstad in
Sweden tackles this by having a heated sand
pit whose temperature is maintained at 50°C.
when the outdoor weather is −5° C. The

most elaborate equipment for children is to be found in parks in the United States, notably in California, often including items such as stockaded forts, railway stations with a locomotive and signals, farms and tractors, or a circus top with wagons. But a trampoline, for example, could easily be provided in every playground and is a success with nearly all children. New York has developed some modular play equipment which needs no foundation and can be quickly assembled or demounted and moved. Canberra's parks department has rightly insisted that besides equipped playgrounds there should also be open space provided for children where they can play with kites, tops or stilts, or make up informal 'blind-man's buff' types of games.

One simple rule is too rarely remembered: to ask the children themselves what they would like — rather than to insist on what the architect or the parks committee think they should like. The involvement of children in their own parks activities is very valuable. Canberra's new Commonwealth Park has an open air amphitheatre whose prime purpose is to encourage impromptu children's plays. In New York children are taught and encouraged to make their own puppet shows and to improvise items from the day's newspapers; a children's theatre and a mobile cinema showing films made by teenagers tour the city; and young volunteers help at day camps in the parks for mentally retarded children. Paris's Jardin d'Acclimatisation, like some American parks, has a popular model road system where children are taught traffic rules in pedal cars and which is run by the

69 These New York mobile playgrounds are valuable, but only the children refuse to be straight lines

police. Sheffield in 1967 started a highly successful annual project when 120 teenage volunteers (from Czechoslovakia, the United States and Ceylon as well as Sheffield) took into the parks over 2,000 children who were living in those areas of the city with inadequate play facilities. Sympathetic supervision is all-important for any project involving children; a few adventure playgrounds are run a little too much like an army assault-course, whereas a good play leader will encourage rather than appear to be organising.

Providing safe play facilities for children should be an urgent social priority. Not only do they keep children happy and off the streets, but also — particularly in twilight slum areas — help to reduce delinquency. The peak crime age in Britain and several other countries is between fifteen and sixteen years old. Here, if it is needed, is a cost-effective argument for adequate parks and playgrounds — it costs £20 to keep one child in an approved school for a week. In New York, more than 70 per cent of the serious crimes are committed by youngsters under 21. Meanwhile bombed sites in London still lie weed-covered and wasted 25 years after the war has ended. But a new generation is growing up for whom future plans will be too late. The immediate crisis is that generally it is the crowded urban areas with the most social problems which are the same ones that have the least amount of open space available. Octavia Hill, who criticised the London School Board for closing their playgrounds in the evenings and at week-ends, pointed out in 1888 that the eastern half of London has only an acre of open space for every 7481 of its residents, whereas the western half had one acre for 682. In London's North Kensington (where Notting Hill is situated) today each child has to share one-tenth of an acre with 88 other children; in richer South Kensington, with only 8. The former area is 152 acres short of open space: but there is no prospect of remedying this, if at all, before several generations of young people have spent their formative years there. Some local parents recently took direct action follow-

ing a child's death in a street accident (a child is knocked down every five days in this area of half a square mile) and invaded locked areas in some squares, clearing away rubbish and establishing their own playgrounds. Stirred, the council allowed a local group to develop some space under a new overhead motorway which had previously been set aside for a car park.

In all there are 25 acres of ground under the motorway between the White City and Paddington; some of its piers, as in a similar scheme at Bristol, serve as divisions between the areas used by children, sport and drama groups. (Tokyo has made intensive use of the area lying under its Central Station bypass, and San Francisco is planning a 2½-mile park under its elevated rapid transit system.) While no substitute for proper open space, such places are useful for noisier activities, and the North Kensington saga is an example of how local initiative, given sufficient determination, can help find an answer to immediate needs.

71 Bowls at Urbino

Some public games have their origin in a more serious contest which gradually became formalised, like the combat between thirty champions apiece from two rival clans which used to be fought on Perth's North Inch. Football has been played on village greens since early times: at Chester the head of an invader was used as a ball. During the seventeenth century Glasgow used to award a prize of twenty shillings for foot races on its Green.

Today, John Blake has recently argued in an article in the *Surveyor,* little effort has yet been made to secure the maximum return on the community's investment in sports facilities through cost-benefit techniques, 'perhaps because it is sensed that such exercises may upset a number of long-cherished beliefs. However, in a situation where land and financial resources are likely to remain limited for many years to come, there is a clear need to ensure not only that the supply of facilities is more closely related to the demand, but also that full value for money is obtained from the large amount of capital already invested in them. This is the real task that faces the various national, regional and local sports councils set up in recent years, and it is one which needs to be tackled as a matter of urgency if Britain is to be able to cope with the effects of the expected "leisure explosion" in the years ahead.'

Such an approach however must not ignore the people interested in minority activities. Idiosyncratic pastimes like punting, skating, ballooning or riding should not be forgotten. Some sports (such as tennis or village cricket) fit much more happily into the ambience of parks than others, whereas model aeroplane-flying for instance can make a peculiarly piercing noise: perhaps there could be separate parks for all activities producing mechanical noises. Compatibility is easier if facilities for the sport are reconcilable with the landscape when they are not in use (e.g. golf — although many courses might be more imaginatively landscaped — whereas squash courts, for instance, are habitually ugly and need not necessarily be sited in parks). Sports halls are today gradually replacing the sacred gymnasia, but some structures are only needed in the winter for sheltering swimming-pools or tennis, netball or basketball courts. Sweden has for several years been using 'air-halls' for this purpose. (These are inflated and erected, without any metal, wood or brick being necessary, in a day, and are kept upright by a fan which circulates warm or cool air. In summertime they can be easily dismantled.) Grouping all the activities round a single social core, as has been done at Billingham, can save expense.

One obvious way in which sport can be

72 Old chalk pit reclaimed as playing fields: Gravesend

each weekend and evening, and other sports fields which belong to companies are only used very rarely by their employees. Wyndham, a co-educational comprehensive school at Egremont in Cumberland, by contrast has pioneered a scheme for real community use which includes the school theatre and public library as well. But the £1 million sports centre at Skelmersdale in Lancashire is inexplicably closed for a month in the summer just when its swimming pool is needed, while the caretakers go on holiday.

Providing additional supervision is far cheaper than duplicating facilities. The problem of the wear of the ground is obviously a limiting factor, but this can be helped by better drainage and tougher blends of grass. Concentrated use is

73 Chalk pit as it might be

provided for many more people without requiring additional land or buildings is to organise the fullest possible public use of the facilities of schools, colleges and universities — including not just the playing fields but also the swimming pools, indoor sports-halls and gymnasia. The best example of this being done at present is in the small Nottinghamshire town of Bingham, where a large sports complex has been jointly planned for school children and public by several of the local councils: mothers can bring their pre-school children to use the teaching pool, for example, during lesson hours — exactly the time that is most convenient for them. But elsewhere, millions of pounds' worth of sports equipment lies wasted for half its useable life considerably easier where the new all-weather playing surfaces have been laid; in parts of the United States plastic grass is used for football pitches, although this is still expensive. Sports equipment — and where useable skis, toboggans and bicycles — could be hired out by enterprising parks departments, so that lack of capital need not prevent anybody from participating.

*   *   *   *   *

There is a double satisfaction in being able to eliminate an eye-sore while adding an amenity at the same time. A good example is the eighty acres of Lancastrian industrial dereliction, known locally as the Wigan Alps, which are being reclaimed in this way to make a totally different road

to Wigan Pier and provide a new sports centre within easy reach of the M6 Motorway. Three high spoil heaps nicknamed the Three Sisters are being converted at a cost of £500,000 to provide ski-slopes, boating and angling, motor-cycle scrambling and an equestrian centre, as well as places for picnicking and rambling. Slag-heaps elsewhere could easily be adapted to provide dry ski runs for learners. After the last war the London County Council created a hundred and ten football pitches at Hackney Marshes by using rubble from London's blitzed buildings as foundations. The Peak Park Planning Board has recently bought 11½ miles of disused railway track in Derbyshire, which after the 12,000 tons of top soil that have been spread on the clinkers have been grass-seeded, will be used for walking and pony trekking. Many other disused railway tracks could be converted in linear parks, such as the proposed 'Wirral Way'; in places where

74 Glasgow band-stand converted into dry ski slope

Skating in the Regent's Park, 1838.

they are too narrow to be used for much else, they could at least provide riding or running tracks.

There is no reason why the Thames, and other urban rivers which are unlikely ever to be pure enough for swimming, should not have floating swimming pools as the Seine does. The excavation of more pools in parks could provide material for hills; in other areas, former quarries could be used. New York has recently opened over sixty 'vest-pocket' pools, primarily in the most neglected areas of the city. The popularity of the Lido in Hyde Park shows the demand of open-air swimmers even in the English climate. (Bathing in the Serpentine until 1930 had been allowed only in the early morning and was restricted to men; George Lansbury, as First Commissioner of Works, over-rode protests to make the Lido there open to women and children throughout the day in the summer). Many outdoor swimming places in parks might be improved by being bordered with clean sand to make a beach, like the large one which has been constructed beside Sloterplas Lake at Amsterdam. In northern countries, much more use would be made

of the water if it were heated and covered with Fuller-type domes or sliding glass or plastic roofs which could be retracted in the summer. In Moscow an open-air pool is kept at a constant temperature of 27° C (81° F), and people swim there even when the air temperature has 50° F of frost. Some places have in addition laid heating cables under sports turf, paths and tennis courts to prevent winter freezing.

Several other ideas are worth considering being adopted more generally. Dry skating rinks in Berlin, used for roller-skating in the summer, are flooded and frozen for ice-skating in the winter; the same could also be done with some paddling-pools and tennis courts. The draughts (checkers) - and chess-tables in Leningrad and New York parks take up little room and are always in use by people of every age, and could be supplemented by a few larger exhibition boards like the one in the square at Crieff in Scotland. And there is a new policy in some American cities of letting tennis courts and swimming pools be used free of charge, since the costs of collection were often found to amount to as much as the receipts.

76 Skiing in a Copenhagen park

77 Battersea Park Sculpture Exhibition

Much has been written elsewhere about the need to make enjoyment of the arts accessible beyond the privileged minorities whose preserve it has been in the past. Some part of many public open spaces could be a forum both for new art-forms and for bringing arts to new audiences — and especially to those people who would not normally consider going into a gallery or a concert-hall. To increase public enjoyment (both active and passive) of the arts is the best long-term way of helping artists. The task is to take the ideas of art out of their cocoon and to show the average family that they can be interesting, controversial and relevant to contemporary life.

Parks as public meeting-places could help to play a role in making art less structured and razing its social barriers — the sense of exclusiveness and subtle snobbery permeating it which segregates it from the majority of the population. Visitors during the weekends and evenings could find themselves unexpectedly able to sample not only bands and prize begonias, but also folk-singing, really well-performed opera and ballet, poetry-reading, modern plays and *al fresco* sculpture, and architectural scale models of new environmental planning. And they should also be able and encouraged to try their own hand at painting or sculpting. Juke-boxes containing (like the one under Times Square) classical, folk and other types of music could have individual earphones to avoid disturbing non-afficionados. Belting out 'Aida' in the Baths of Caracalla or Verona's Arena may have made some opera-singers hoarse, but they are marvellous settings in which to introduce several thousand people to at least a certain kind of opera. Other park areas could act as a temporary campus for experiments in mixed media which could help to abolish the compartmental boundaries between different arts. As with sports, temporary structures of style (in fibreglass or other materials) could be put up to shelter winter events. Each park should mount its own annual festival by and for its neighbourhood. Profits from events could go to charities or encouraging local arts.

There are some successful initiatives already. The sculpture exhibitions in Battersea Park gained an international reputation, and it is regrettable that the G.L.C. economised by cancelling the 1969 one.

The open-air concerts at the Shell in Boston draw thousands of city-workers on summer evenings. In 1969, a third of a million young people attended a pop concert in Hyde Park — reputedly the largest open-air meeting since the Chartists, yet causing less vandalism or litter than many football matches. Open-air

78 Hanover park theatre of 1800

79 Hanover theatre and park today

plays at Holland Park merge with the sounds of cricket-bats and the cries of the peacocks in the gardens. On fine evenings in New York and London, outdoor Shakespeare survives despite the competition of midges and aeroplanes. The setting of the classical concerts at Kenwood is unbelievably lyrical and escapist for so near the centre of London: the Pastoral Symphony comes across the water blending with the sounds of waterfowls against a stupendous backdrop of beech and elm woods; as dusk falls people lie on the grass and watch the stars appear, as they do listening to the music festival at Tanglewood in Massachusetts.

In several cities the local museum and art gallery are sited inside the park, but there is no institution more in need of the removal of the walls that separate them from the public. Their contents' relevance to contemporary life and art needs to be visibly demonstrated; as far as security allows, walls could be made of transparent plastic in order to intrigue and tempt inside new viewers who would not ordinarily think of entering. New York is planning to send mobile art museums into slum areas of the city. 'The traditional museum *aux musées :* why should commercial emporia

have all the best window displays?

Considering that museums and galleries are maintained by tax and ratepayers for enjoyment why should most of them be so lugubrious? Their contents should be de facto as well as theoretically accessible to everybody who wishes to see them: each museum and gallery should have a creche and playroom where children could be left with an attendant and where there are objects they can touch. Whether in parks or not, they should moreover be open in the early evening and throughout weekends, even if this means closing on weekday mornings. How many of them make use of surrounding gardens and courtyards for fountains or sculpture? By planning special activities for

80 Concert on a summer night in a London park: Kenwood
81 Museum in the park

museum in the park

the winter months the ones inside park boundaries could help to make parks used more evenly throughout the year.

Mexico City's museums are some of the best in the world through their feeling of freedom and interdisciplinary use of open-plan display. The new Pitt-Rivers museum which may be built by Nervi and Powell and Moya at Oxford is planned to have roof gardens as well as cycles of different temperatures and humidities for plants and trees to act as living settings for the anthropological exhibits. Several countries have created interesting open-air historical museums with carefully restored buildings from former eras. Norway, Sweden, Ireland and Finland have folk museums with houses that show their old architectural styles (Skausen at Stockholm is particularly good); in the United States at Mystic, Connecticut, a whaling seaport is preserved. £6 million of Rockefeller money has brilliantly reconstructed Williamsburg, Virginia as it was in its Colonial days; and even an old street of shops can make an interesting display as it does at York. Park-museums containing historical industrial exhibits should also be laid out. Many historic buildings, such as tithe barns, could come into their own again if they were used for selected events instead of being regarded as decaying exhibits. Caerphilly Castle has recently gained a new life through being used by the surrounding community, including youth and arts groups: local schools helped to restore the grounds, and vandalism there is now negligible.

For those with different interests

82 Zahndam, Holland. Old houses and windmills rebuilt in the park

London's Alexandra and Crystal Palaces, each in their own park, could be made into stately pleasure-domes or Fun Palaces respectively for the north and south of the Thames — if good transport connections were provided. One of the factors wrong with Battersea Pleasure Gardens is the poor access by public transport.

Planners should always beware lest they prescribe not what people want, but what the planners think they should want.

Nevertheless, the popularity of Copenhagen's Tivoli Gardens and Vienna's Prater, both in a similar climate, show the potential which Battersea and Coney Island miss. Tivoli was built by an admirer of Vauxhall Gardens, and we should now return the compliment. With Oistrakh and Sammy Davis playing in successive weeks, Tivoli succeeds in pulling in the hotdog and the scampi sets side by side. Designed to look as good by day as by night, it preserves a style and gaiety which echo the descriptions of Vauxhall's balloon ascents, waterfalls, fireworks, outdoor pantomime, and entry tickets designed by Hogarth. At Tivoli hostesses look after children in playcorners without charge. With its cabarets, ballet, mime and concerts, it is a place where adults can feel at home, whereas most equivalent places in America seem geared exclusively to children and the Disney cult. The Vidam in Budapest and the People's Parks in Leningrad are better; despite the puritanism which East European countries share with the United States, family excursions in the former seem to be not so totally dominated by children's standards (although there are carriages with toys specially for children in some Russian trains). The Linnanmaki Park at Helsinki has the excellent idea of devoting the profits of its funfair (some £40,000 annually since it opened in 1950) to six children's charities. Such profits could equally well be used to provide children's parks and playgrounds in areas where they are needed, perhaps with facilities for creating art in its various forms.

New York's ethnic groups hold their

83 Fireworks at Tivoli, Copenhagen

local block festivals, when streets are closed off for a day, and stalls, amusements and dance bands create lively carnivals. Joan Littlewood, whose proposal for a large Fun Palace for East London has not yet been given support, also suggested that there should be small experimental arts laboratories on several under-used patches of ground at street-corners and crossroads. 'Take a diverse gang, team or party of local citizens with specialised skills, decide what is most needed in this microcosm and transform jejune plot into launch pad,' she advised in the *Architects' Journal,* 'I guarantee that during process said citizens will experience fascinating identity, sex or skill change.' In the 1968 City of London Festival she was allowed to try her hand at a mobile fair, and near the Tower she put up a giant human body for people to enter, space and underwater trips designed by members of the Architectural Association, a fibreglass modular playground, inflated clouds and 'bouncing walls'. The same Festival saw 130 modern sculptures placed in the traditionally grey streets of London's 'Square Mile', as a vigorous example of the policy which is being attempted in several cities of getting art out of the holiness of galleries and into some relationship with people's daily lives. Exhibitions and displays should be mounted where people are,

such as the concourses of airports and railway stations. One means suggested as a way of helping to do this is by 'Pavilions in the Parks': temporary inflatable structures in which contemporary films, art, music, sculpture and poetry can easily be moved to different parks and street-corners. Some similar form of liveliness and gaiety needs to be added to cultural ghettoes like the Lincoln Centre or London's South Bank. In New York a Movie Bus circulates throughout the city showing films made by teenagers for teenagers. Cuba has travelling cinemas mounted on lorries. Best of all of course is to allow people themselves through the barrier to participate: there could be do-it-yourself artist's corners with clay, chalks, paint, paper and canvas available in parks to parallel Hyde Park's Speakers' Corner.

84 Artists' do-it-yourself corner

10 New Parks. 'No city should be too large for a man to walk out of in a morning.' — *The Unquiet Grave*

Proper provision for children, sports and arts will require new space, if the peace of existing parks is to be safeguarded — and, preferably, extended. In the current pressure on urban living space, where can such areas be found? A new park is regrettably rare. Newcastle's Town Moor and London's Lee Valley are two plans to provide new recreational areas, but most cities make increasingly crowded use of the legacies of their past without adding any new contribution for the future. Opportunities to plan anything imaginative have been missed in the post-war reconstruction and slum-clearance of many grey areas. For a considerable time, the provision of new parks has been at a slower rate than the growth in population, without beginning to take account of the rapid expansion in the demand for recreation. (For instance, Illinois, which now has five per cent of the United States' population, possesses only 0.05 per cent of the recreational land.)

Little built-on land is likely to revert to open space, but one way to meet the deficiencies is by improving the amenity value of the existing land which has not been built over. There are considerable opportunities which have been opened up by new legislation in the 1.25 million acres of commons in England and Wales. The potentialities of green belts have only been very cursorily realized: barely one-twentieth of London's green belt is at present used for recreation. One suggestion which has been made is that London should build on 40,000 acres of its green belt and create an equivalent 40,000 acres of new parks within its conurbation; but in any event more positive planning could vastly improve the amenity and recreational use of land in the belt. No other source of open space land should be left unexplored — including the 3,700 acres which the Ministry of Defence and the 4,200 acres which the Department of Health and Social Security hold in London. Some of the grounds possessed by both general and mental hospitals could be shared with the community, to the mutual benefit of the people in both. Several prisons might well be resited in more modern buildings outside central urban areas. 83 acres of inner London are taken up by five prisons; Islington in particular needs the sites of Pentonville and Holloway for housing and parks. The armed forces are now using 700,000 acres of land in Britain, including 145 miles of our coast, compared with only 225,000 acres before the last war. Recreation has always been the Cinderella of land use.

In Britain there are between 150,000 and 250,000 acres of land (depending on the definition of dereliction) which are squandered because they are derelict, in-

cluding at least 36,000 acres in heavily
populated urban areas — and this is being
added to by over 3,000 acres a year. In the
Potteries district alone there are 9,000
derelict acres, whose neglect is hard to ex-
cuse in the face of the shortage of
recreational land in the area. Since 1966,
the central government makes a grant of
fifty per cent, rising to eighty-five per cent
in development areas, towards the cost of
reclamation of derelict land, but the annual
rate of reclamation is at present less than

86 North Kensington - even London has large areas
without green space

2,000 acres throughout the country. A
great deal of derelict land could be flooded
for recreational use as well as water sup-
plies — thereby also saving the unspoilt
moors and valleys being taken elsewhere.
Mention has been made earlier of one example, the development of wet gravel pits
into lakes at Wraysbury, which is likely to

be a highly successful commercial venture although it will be a pity if they become reserved for clubs instead of being open to the public. Gordon Cullen, the landscape consultant, is proposing to take advantage of the silt that is left after the washing of the gravel to break the monotony of the form and standard depth of excavation by planting shrubs and reeds. Just as we owe the Broads to peat-digging six centuries ago, Chasewater in Staffordshire has become another popular water park; but there are many other opportunities (such as former limestone and slate quarries, and the worked-out chalk pits on the Kent side of the Thames estuary) which are not being put to use. Only seven of the sixty reservoirs in the Peak District National Park are used for recreation; reclaimed estuaries could provide several kinds of both wet and dry parks. Blue belts could be added to green belts: lagoons can supply the needs of swimmers, anglers or sailing dinghies — or just agreeable decoration

87 Dereliction: Lancashire

88 Dereliction converted

with swans and waterfowl. Besides water-parks, so far there are few really good water-gardens anywhere in Britain; but the mariachis and markets of Mexico's Xochimilco show how alive a lake-park can be, and Japan is now developing 'under-water parks' on its Pacific coast, with glass-bottomed boats, underwater observation towers and restaurants, and the water illu-minated at night.

In the search for future parkland no material however unpromising should be despised. The lush 1,117 acres of San Francisco's Golden Gate Park were created out of what were formerly sand-dunes. The Backs at Cambridge were raised on rubble in the Middle Ages, just as the sports fields at Hackney Marshes were laid out after the last war on a base of ten feet of rubble from the London blitz. Every city has

enough spoil to make Silbury Hills in its parks if it wishes. Berlin used 30 million cubic metres of its rubble after the last war for making recreational hills in the city. Napoleon III conjured the romantic master-piece of Paris' Buttes-Chaumont Park out of a former sewage pit and abandoned gypsum workings in 1864-7: despite the high towers now visible round its edge, it still forms a fantastic escapist opera-set in the middle of the city, like a trap-door out of modern life. The site of the luxuriant little park by the Pope's palace at Avignon was bare rock until it was covered with soil from road-excavations; Battery Park in New York is built on land which was man-made in 1870. Battersea Park was created from a marsh of the Thames with the help of earth dredged from London's docks, and its mounds formed by the material taken from the excavation of its own lake and from Cubitt's new housing estate in Belgravia.

Modern earth-moving techniques and soil-making science have transformed the possibilities of what can be done with derelict land. New York's 1,200-acre Flushing Meadow was laid out on an un- promising site of tidal swamp and a rubbish dump, and at present the City is working on turning Jamaica Bay into a 15,000-acre nature reserve. At Wilmington in County Durham a 190-foot high pit heap has been converted into thirty acres of green fields. Whereas full reclamation remains expensive, costing about £700 an acre, cosmetic im-

89 Park from sewage pit - Buttes de Chaumont, Paris

90 Coal tips, County Durham

provement can be achieved for only
£50-100 an acre. Tips and spoil-heaps do
not as was once thought invariably have to
be levelled but can provide undulating
wooded walks and features in the landscape at a much lower cost.

Linear parks, which provide at least
maximal access if little scope for design,
can be created comparatively simply from
obsolete urban features such as former railway and tram tracks, canals and aqueducts.
In addition they can be used to provide
valuable pedestrian links between larger
open spaces.

Even where there is not an inch of derelict land available, parks can still be made
on the roofs of buildings — which, as
Lancelot Brown would have said, have
great capabilities. The city of Foustat in
Egypt used to have orchards and gardens
all over the roofs of its warren of houses.
High densities today are resulting, Tony
Southart points out, in an increasing
number of people looking down on cities
from their homes and offices. Derry and
Toms' store, built in 1938, showed that

91 Transformation of tips into wooded hills
92 The possibilities of roofs: Derry and Toms, London

there is no reason why trees should not be successfully established in a roof garden. The silence of some roof gardens with no overlooking buildings, high above the pandemonium of the traffic, can create a feeling not unlike being in a walled garden in the country. Lower roof gardens with their silhouettes of foliage can provide visual interest which is welcome in cities. At Hartford (Connecticut) a four-acre pedestrian area over car-parks and service areas has been planted with shrubs; the

Kaiser Centre at Oakland (California) has on its roof a complete small park including a lake, grass and trees. The roof garden and trees of the Grosse Schanze on top of the railway station at Berne show the opportunity which has been lost through wasting the large flat roof of London's Euston Station and the tops of low modern school buildings and airports (where islands of relaxation are particularly necessary).

Japan and the United States have come to realise that miniature parks (like Bryant Park which makes a cool oasis in the middle of Manhattan) can have a value out of all proportion to the size of their site: where space is limited, some towns could consider making a Japanese-style concentrated type of garden.

Many housing estates being built today lag behind the requirements of the resolution introduced by Hume in the House of Commons in 1838 that all enclosure Bills must provide adequate open space for the exercise and recreation of the neighbourhood. The huge estate at Clifton outside Nottingham for instance is seriously deficient; but at Hattersley, near Hyde, a 50-acre ravine running through the centre of a new overspill development has been left as a natural picnic area. One idea which has received mixed criticism is the development of 'leisure' or 'chalet' gardens, which have become popular in Germany, Holland and Scandinavia and are now being tried at Cardiff. Generally situated on the edge of densely populated areas, these consist of between 40 and 400 plots each with a chalet which the local authority sells or leases to town families.

At Rotterdam, they are combined with a recreational complex which includes areas for children and sport. Like allotments, chalet gardens rarely improve visual landscape, but they undoubtedly fill a need and give much pleasure, especially to families living in flats; possibly they could be landscaped with tree-planting. Hamburg has a 600-acre area of weekend homes which have been successfully merged among successfully woods planted in reclaimed gravel workings.

*   *   *   *

More than 25,000 acres of land in Great Britain are at present occupied by cemeteries, and this limbo is increasing by some 500 further acres each year. Lewis Mumford (who once described civilisation's cycle as being a sequence of Metropolis, Megapolis, Tyrannopolis, Necropolis) urged the removal of tombstones and the conversion of their area into parks — pointing out that, not for the first time in history, the dead were being abundantly supplied with necessities of life which are denied to the quick. In the United States half a million acres, increasing by several thousand a year, have been covered by cemeteries, nearly all in or near urban areas: a total approximately equivalent to that of all the cities' parks. Liverpool, Manchester and several parts of London and other old cities are estimated now to have a rather greater population occupying places in their cemeteries than they contain of living inhabitants. 3,120 acres in Greater London are taken up by ceme-

93 Liverpool park in an old cemetery

teries, and a further 490 acres are earmarked for burial grounds. In the Queens area of New York they form the bulk of the open space. Some cemeteries do in fact contribute a romantic form of park, such as the famous one at Highgate (described by Ian Nairn as a gently deliquescent exercise in stucco horror); or Liverpool's St. James's whose wilderness of Piranesian ramps, tunnels and catacombs, constructed on an awesome scale in 1827 from a disused stone quarry, is used as a natural adventure playground by children — although at present it lies under threat of being 'municipalised'.

Less interesting cemeteries can be converted into open space 50 years after their last interment. The famous Washington Square in New York besides being the site of a cemetery where 10,000 people were buried was once (like Marble Arch and the acacias of Prague's Loretta Square) a place for executions — another source of open space for which we should be grateful because of people's reluctance to build there. In London, 29 acres of Tower

Hamlets cemetery and 18 at Birchen Grove (Brent) are at present being deconsecrated, but many others such as the one at Kensal Green could usefully follow. At Nunhead, for example, fifty-two acres of former graves — an area of open space as large as Mayfair — lie crumbling and overgrown, padlocked for most of the time, less than 5 miles from the centre of London.

St. Pancras is a good example of what can be done to make an old churchyard into a pleasing haven from traffic. A general enabling Act of Parliament has now made much easier the procedure for conversion, which used to require an individual Act in each case besides interminable efforts to trace descendants of the graveholders. Since every 1,000 cremations result in the saving of at least an acre of land in Britain and far more in America, it might be worth subsidising cremation with free funerals to prevent the prospect of the countryside slowly being covered with marble inscriptions and granite chips. (Even without subsidy, a cremation costs only £9 compared with an average of £30 for a burial. In 1967 cremation formed 49 per cent of all funerals in Britain — 55 per cent in London — and now that it is officially permitted for Roman Catholics, it is increasing by some 2 per cent a year.) Muslim countries have a slight advantage over Christian ones in respect of the ground their cemeteries occupy, because they bury their dead vertically; but it would save more scarce land if more parishes adopted the Mediterranean practice of stacking graves in walls.

*   *   *   *

With competition for land so intense, it is necessary to try to plan wherever possible for its multiple use. The Tennessee Valley Authority in the United States was a pioneering example of reconciling the dual provision of power and recreation. In Britain, walkers are unfortunately denied access to some of its most beautiful areas — such as the Forest of Bowland and parts of Snowdonia and Yorkshire — but Grizedale Forest and the Forest of Dean show how farming, forestry and recreation can coexist successfully. Gora, India's leading atheist, uprooted ornamental plants in a Delhi park and planted vegetables instead. Chelmsford produces crops of willows for cricket-bats from one of its town parks; many towns' derelict areas and bomb-sites could have contributed toward the cost of their conversion by being planted with crops of trees. The ever-increasing spread of golf-courses is another area where one function could be combined with selected silviculture — as well as better landscaping. Forest parks with camping sites could also be set up in the green belts of major cities: woods are good at absorbing crowds and serving as sponges to soak people in off the roads.

Local authorities — including urban ones — in Britain are now given powers by the new Countryside Act to establish various forms of country parks, and can be helped by a grant from the Countryside Commission of 75 per cent of the cost. Such parks will obviously be doubly valuable if they can be set up as near as possible to urban centres. Over 100,000 people in a recent Whit weekend visited the

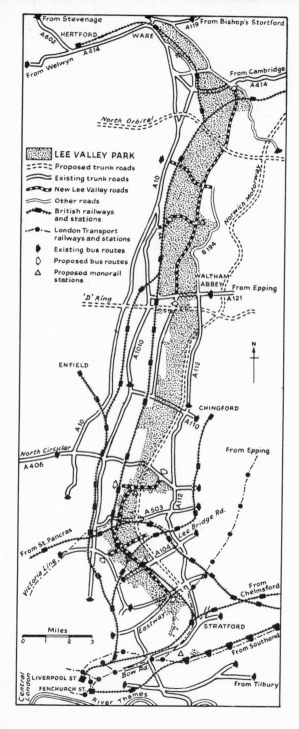

National Trust's Clumber Park, one of the former ducal estates lying between Sheffield and Nottingham. Hampshire County Council, which has acquired 2,000 acres and provided 23 open spaces with picnic and parking areas, strongly advocates the public ownership of open spaces which it describes as "socially desirable and fully justified by results". Since people are likely in future to travel further and be more selective, sometimes groups of local authorities could pool their resources, as several councils between Manchester and Bolton are considering doing to create a joint linear park along ten miles of the Croal and Irwell valleys. A recent survey showed that a quarter of the car owners in London had made a journey on the previous Sunday: yet London is at the moment particularly badly placed in not having any National Park nearer than the Peak District — a good hundred and twenty miles and several hours — distant. Britain has a great deal to do before her roads have picnic areas of the standard of some of those in the United States and Canada or on the new French motorway south from Paris.

The creation of 'magnet' or 'honeypot' parks as near as possible to conurbations would help to siphon off congestion and reduce the lemming-like traffic jams on roads to the coasts which at the moment are our chief recreation area. When the Lee Valley regional park is complete in 1985, it is estimated that a million people will

94 The future Lee Valley Regional Park, London

visit it at weekends. This is planned to provide a wide variety of recreation linearly over 6,000 acres in the valley of the River Lee, London's second river but at present an inglorious sight. At Picketts Lock, for example, one of the recreation centres that is planned for inside the park, there will be a sports hall, ice rink, lido bathing-pool, golf course, an all-weather games pitches with flood-lighting, a sauna and a restaurant.

Abercrombie had seen in the Lee Valley the opportunity for his 'green-wedge' idea of bringing fingers of the countryside into the heart of the city, like the Bois de la Cambre in Brussels. Similar schemes to the Lee and Colne Valley Parks could benefit the conurbations in the Tyne and Trent valleys.

Popular 'honey-pots' will help to preserve the solitude of other parks for those who seek peace and quiet. As new roads have made them easily accessible to millions more motorists, places like the Yorkshire Dales, the Cornish Coast and the Lake District are approaching saturation point. When the motorway system is completed, there will be 5 million people within an hour's drive of the Dales National Park, and 16 million within two hours. Germany now has 48 vehicles for every mile of her roads; Italy, 45. If all Britain's cars came out on the roads together, they would have 11 yards of road each; by 1980, this will be down to seven yards. If more roads are created in response to this, then there will in turn be less unspoilt countryside to visit. But a new park is cheaper than a new highway as a means for relieving the pres-

sure on the seaside and coping with the centrifugal urge to fly from the city. Most North American cities have a regional park near to them. As future traffic growth will annually make unspoilt countryside less and less accessible to city dwellers, it is sensible in economic (as well as in visual and social) terms to provide as close at hand as possible the rural satisfactions that attract us to the country — the quiet; haystacks, woods, streams and waterfalls; places to picnic and explore; village cricket and pubs; and even a few farms, which would especially be enjoyed by town children. People of exemplary patience would be needed to run such farms and they will be unlikely to make much profit, but cities could support them to show ploughing, harvesting, and cattle, horses and sheep as well as crops. It might be possible to arrange for local urban comprehensive schools to adopt and run a farm each. Manchester's Heaton Park is one of several which could be extended into adjoining farmland. Sir Frederick Gibberd planned wedges of farmland to run into his Harlow new town. Stockholm since as long ago as 1906 has been following a policy of buying up the farms which surround it and leasing them to farmers, and Manchester has recently reared Highland and Belted Galloway cattle in its parks. The Rhineland

existing trees continued out into square

cars removed and paved square formed

cities have bought and run the farms which remain in their areas, as part of a recreational network of unspoilt country which the Ruhr Valley Authority has been saving in the middle of such a heavily industrialised district since the 1920s, and which includes the preservation of forests to mask some of the factories.

'Nature trails' have become very popular and over a hundred have now been established in Britain, although unfortunately once again none is in or very near to London. Among the first was Linn Park in Glasgow, and both there and Birmingham produce excellent illustrated guides on what to look for. The first nature reserve to be created by law anywhere in the world was in part of the Forest of Fontainebleau in 1858. The Yosemite Valley was saved six years later; Yellowstone in 1872 was the first to be known as a 'national park'. It may become necessary to control admission, but although in any conflict of interests the needs of the fauna and flora must be paramount, 30,000 people were for instance able to see the ospreys nesting near Loch Garten through binoculars from a hide. Shell Oil has recently helped with finance to set up a new nature trail in Plym Bridge Woods, a beautiful valley less than 5 miles from Plymouth's centre which was recently saved for the public by a £7,500 appeal organised by the National Trust. The number of visitors to the bird sanctuaries of Aubrey Buxton at Stansted and Peter Scott at Slimbridge show that there is an insatiable demand for such places in Britain — and of course the more they are visited, the larger the area that is needed for the sake of the wild life. The London Natural History Society, reporting that foxes had recently arrived at Wimbledon Common and Wembley Park, wondered whether some animals were being driven to take refuge in towns by the hordes of field study groups. Whether because of this or because of the Clean Air Act, fauna seem now definitely to be on the increase in some cities. There are two sets of badgers in Richmond Park; a fox was found to have collected eight golf balls from a Ruislip course; and 138 different species of birds, more than ever before, have been noted in London's Royal parks. The latter are tended with fanatical care: the question of whether there was an excessive drake mallard population in St. James's Park was solemnly considered by a special committee following complaints from people distressed by the spectacle of mating rivalry and pursuits. And when a pair of herons in 1968 nested for the first time in a London park, the *Times* gave the news more space than it gives in a year to the several thousand homeless human families in London.

97 Canals - a little money and care could make a lot of difference

Cities' rivers and canals are their most neglected assets. Watersides can provide the
largest amount of recreation with the least
cost to land; but Cleveland (Ohio)'s river
Cuyahoga is so contaminated with oil that
it has become the only known piece of
water to be classified as a fire-hazard. The
Mersey, the Irwell and the Yorkshire Don
are so full of sewage and industrial effluent
that no animal can drink or bathe in them
without risk of death.

Rochdale is planning a linear waterside
park along its canals, but the wasted opportunities of the Thames and the Tyne have

been lamented for centuries, without any action ever seeming to follow. Why shouldn't other cities have water-taxis, *bateaux-mouches* like Paris, the *rondvaart boten* of Amsterdam, the pretty floating restaurants of Leningrad? Many people in Stockholm travel to work by boat. Why can't London have hovercraft and hydrofoils, as regular as Venice's vaporetti, to link the City, Westminster, the South Bank and Waterloo? London Transport possesses the powers to run such services but has never done so. Michael Young and Peter Willmott's Thameside Research and Development Group suggests that the produce for the new Nine Elms and Billingsgate Markets could come by water, thus saving traffic-jams. Why couldn't there also be floating markets like in Bangkok and Mexico? At Xochimilco Mexican families happily punt between man-made islands of vegetables and flowers which are growing on floating islands in a water-park.

Glasgow could similarly do much to improve its rivers: the Clyde, the Kelvin and the Leven. In earlier times the Thames used to form the centre of London's life. This was helped by its bed then being shallower and wider, and by the nineteen piers of the old London Bridge which by acting as an effective weir restricted the tidal rise and fall of the water-level upstream. The key to having recreational lagoons and marinas in the Thames today would be to build a new barrage or dam somewhere near Woolwich — as has in fact been proposed ever since 1790. (The barrage at Boston [Mass.] has made the river Charles both more decorative and more navigable). Varieties

of old ships could be berthed in rivers to provide historic floating museums.

At present the general popular belief is that the only things one is likely to catch in the Thames or in the rivers of many cities are typhoid or pneumonia. In fact recent cleaning of the water has resulted in the Thames now having shrimps at Canvey Island and roach, eels and bream as far as Fulham for the first time this century. Sweden has invented a new technique for reclaiming water by pumping air along its bed. But the County of London Plan of 1943 showed that only 3.6 miles (9 per cent) of London's 39.3 miles of Thames bankside were public open space, compared with the 28.9 miles (73 per cent) taken by industry, warehouses and wharves. Abercrombie proposed that 11.7 miles (30 per cent) should be open public space and this was a very modest suggestion, since Berlin has laid out for the public over one-third of its waterside. But instead since then the Bankside power-station has been built, and even more recently a huge multi-storey car park near the water is providing empty cars with an excellent view of the river by the Monument. The potentialities of the tributaries of the Thames in London — the Beam, Beverley Brook, Brent, Colne, Crane, Cray-Darent, Hogsmill, Ingrebourne, Lee, Ravensbourne, Roding and Wandle — are equally wasted.

The chance of rectifying much of this is — probably for the last time — now presented to us. The Mermaid Theatre and Restaurant have shown what can be made from one old riverside warehouse. The container revolution is at present in the process of making many miles of docks redundant. The area of dockland rendered obsolete has briefly given every port the most comprehensive development opportunity in its history. London, confronted with a planning chance greater than that following the Blitz, has for example St. Katherine's Dock on a site of 15 acres of land and 10 acres of water which may be transformed into an outstanding amenity, arts or tourist centre, lying as it is just by the Tower of London. San Francisco has demonstrated the way: the sensitive adaptations of the former in-

dustrial buildings of The Cannery and Ghirardelli Square are ahead of anywhere else — but could be followed in fifty decaying docklands. At Ghirardelli, an old chocolate factory has been made by William Murster into the centre of a complex of multi-level traffic-free courtyards, shops, gardens and cafes which is both socially alive and a financial success. New varieties of enterprise are being added to those already open, which include six restaurants, two art galleries and a theatre. At the nearby Cannery, Leonard Martin has cunningly fitted out a former fruit-canning plant with escalators, esplanades and walk-

98 Canalside walk

The Swan

pub overlooking canal

road behind wall

Bass

canal

canalside walk protected from traffic by wall

ways. The detailing of both is excellent. Although both centres, being private commercial enterprises, tend to cater rather too much for the trendy boutique set, they are as environments model successes. Boston, Belfast, Hamburg, Liverpool, Hull, Glasgow, Bristol, New Orleans, New York and London, please copy — perhaps with more informal joint public-private development, facilities to cater for all tastes, and mixed-income village communities living in the dockspace.

*   *   *   *   *

Similar imagination could make amenity assets of urban canals, which too often are sealed away behind blank walls and barbed wire. Towpaths offer the opportunity of a network of traffic-free walks across cities and they could inter-link with nearby open spaces. Warrington's canals might be used like Amsterdam's with trees planted along the banks; and John Betjeman has pointed out that Birmingham has a greater length of canal than Venice. Even though they may never resemble Venice or Udaipur, linear parks could be laid out along them: Derek Lovejoy has produced a plan for a canal park walk along several miles of Rochdale's canals which at present are an ugly as well as a dangerous hazard. London has some 58 miles of canal, but they are largely hidden from view and falling into dereliction being used as dumping grounds and becoming deserted death-traps for children. A group of enthusiasts have shown by a pilot study how the Regent's Canal could be made into a linear park for both walking and boating through some of the most in-

dustrial parts of London. Alan Brien, who has suggested that we find the sound of water soothing because of memories of the first nine months of our existence, wrote: 'The water is there in and around all our great cities . . . . but usually hidden away. For centuries, we treated our streams as sewers. Passers-by are only reminded that they inhabit an archipelago of brick islands when they glimpse the canals and waterways from the top deck of a bus'.

*   *   *   *   *

Parks alongside rivers and canals also need cafes and restaurants for walkers. But the catering in most public open spaces is too often memorable only for its lack of imagination and cleanliness. If you want to

99 Hyde Park restaurant

eat in all except a handful of parks — take a picnic. Jeremy Bugler states that one cafe in a south London park reminds him of the set of Pinter's *'The Caretaker'.* Patrick Gwynne's imaginative designs for the two new restaurants at either end of the Serpentine in Hyde Park show that there is no reason why this should be so (although it is a pity that it isn't the tables instead of the kitchens of the western restaurant that look out over the water). But most snack-bar fare is typical motorway stuff at monopoly prices. And why aren't there cafe chairs and tables under trees and umbrellas, for the footsore tourists in Leicester Square or Trafalgar Square? The surrounding traffic could be mitigated by being sunk in cuttings lined with trees. Tourist spas such as Bath, Cheltenham, Harrogate and Buxton in particular need such improvements. And now that it has been closed to traffic at weekends, why shouldn't there be cafes under awnings all along the Mall terrace vying with each other like those

100 Al fresco life: Avignon cafe under the trees

lining the Piazza San Marco? At least one restaurant should be sited on the edge of most parks, looking out over it. Glass-screens, hot-air curtains and infra-red heating could result in much more eating, drinking or sitting out for most months in the year even in northern parks. Our licencing laws should be dragged into the twentieth-century so that they could help to unite, not split up the family. Temporary food-kiosks, attractively designed, could adapt their menus and be moved around according to seasons. The more variety there is, the better: visitors to parks should be able to buy both cheese and beer or salmon and Chablis. Clement Freud showed what can be done at the open-air theatre's restaurant in Regent's Park. The elegant restaurants of the Bois are too exclusively aristocratic for most Parisians; but Tivoli has no less than twenty-two different restaurants — including six that are among the best in Copenhagen. And why shouldn't we also be allowed to dance under the sky in summer?

101 Open air dance floor

open air dance floor — set in hollow surrounded by trees

'It's all very well making suggestions, but how will they be paid for?' The cost of parks is rising in any event. New York's budget for running them was $6m. in 1934 but was $40.2m. by 1965/6, $42.6m. for 1966/7, $52.5m. for 1967/8 and $57m. for 1968/9. The capital outlay of New York on its parks rose as dramatically as his helium balloons when Tom Hoving was Commissioner:

1965/6	:	$22.1 million
1966/7	:	$28.2 million
1967/8	:	$51.5 million
1968/9	:	$18.0 million

London's budget has risen less rapidly. In 1967/8 the Greater London Council's parks' running costs were £4,841,494 (set off by an income from them of £626,162) and had capital expenditure of £898,665. The following year the total expenditure on parks and the Thames was £5,032,000 (offset by £630,000) and for 1969/70, £5,170,500. The royal parks in London and Edinburgh cost the central government's Ministry of Public Building and Works £1,800,000 in 1968/9 (compared with £877,000 in 1958/9). The annual spending by the individual London borough councils in 1965/6 ranged from Barnet's £495,552 on its 1,654 acres and Hillingdon's £296,688 on its 2,923 acres down to Hackney's £72,184 on its 20 acres and wealthy Kensington and Chelsea's Scrooge-like £43,917 on its 79 acres.

The total expenditure on 'parks, pleasure grounds and open spaces' by councils in Great Britain in 1966/7 (the latest financial year for which full returns are available) was:

£ millions:	Gross	Net
		(i.e. less takings)
England:	44.4	38.0
(including London:	8.4	7.8)
Scotland:	6.0	5.1
Wales:	2.5	2.2

Northern Ireland spent £740,000 in 1967/8, compared with £650,000 in 1966/7.

An expenditure of slightly over a pound annually per head of population was fairly consistent in most urban areas in Britain:

County Borough	Net Expenditure '66/7	Population 1966	Expenditure per head of population	Capital Expenditure
Birmingham	£1,279,661	1,102,570	23/-	£37,881
Liverpool	£831,767	712,040	23/4	£155,642
Manchester	£769,863	625,250	24/7	£60,042

This compares with, for example, about DM:45 per inhabitant annually in Berlin.

Councils on the whole are shy of publicising the cost of parks; but if they did so it might possibly increase public appreciation of them. John Barr, in his excellent Pelican, points out that the national expenditure on pets or gardening would serve to reclaim all the derelict land in the country within one year, and proposes that extractive developers should finance reclamation by a levy on the lines of the successful Ironstone Restoration Fund. On all its National (countryside) Parks, Britain is at present spending only a sum equivalent to the cost of a cigarette for each person in the population. Would it not be healthier if we spent on our urban and country parks a sum nearer to the total spent on smoking (currently some £1,500 millions a year)?

The Greek Chamber of Technology has warned that in 10 years' time, every inhabitant of Athens will have to pay £25 a year to cover the cost of filtering the atmosphere if measures — including increasing the area of trees and open space in the city — are not taken. The total annual bill would be £76 millions. 'If we fail to act immediately' their report con-

cludes 'it will be difficult for the Greek economy to afford such a sum for Athens alone, and there would be no other solution than for the population to abandon the city.'

The Treasury should note that outstanding parks attract the foreign currency of tourist revenue: American visitors often say that the parks are what they most admired about London. Nevertheless, with so many other priorities competing for councils' money, it would be unrealistic to expect any large increase in the proportion of the budget devoted to open spaces. Not that the staff of parks are paid extravagantly: the take-home pay of £11. 8. 8d. a week of a labourer in a London park, compared with manual workers' average earnings of £23 a week, put him among the lowest paid workers in the country. It meant in one recent case that an employee had after paying his rent less than £6 a week with which to feed and clothe himself, his wife and child, and to heat and light his home and pay all other living expenses. It is hardly surprising that graduates or even O-levels are extremely rare. The turnover of parks staff in Manchester runs at an average of 50 per cent; in one area the department lost 94 per cent of its staff in a single year. Birmingham lost 413 out of its staff of 1100 in 1968; Glasgow lost more than 500. Many departments are reduced to relying on a shifting supply of unskilled labour, though pay is rising.

Some of the most labour-intensive features of parks, such as floral clocks, fence-painting and meticulously weeded flowerbeds, could be reduced; or, if the neighbouring community strongly desired them local volunteers could help with their upkeep. Many frustrated town people enjoy gardening, and money saved in this way could be used to create new parks in areas which badly need them. It has already been argued that providing these is cheaper than building ever-wider motorways for people in search of recreation; and that some amenities such as forestry, golf-courses and sailing lagoons can be financially profitable and help to subsidise uncommercial ones. The nylon ski-slope at Crystal Palace for example makes money for the G.L.C.: why are there not more elsewhere? Demand has begun to outrun the supply of flooded gravel-pits near large cities; the new reservoir at Grafham has a turnover of £40,000 a year from fishing and a closed waiting list of 500 for its sailing club only two years after its opening. In any event, the responsibility for the reclamation of derelict land should be borne by the relevant industry, and not by the public.

The cost of traffic-free pedestrian routes in cities, of which open spaces form a part, are offset by several savings. The reduction of accidents and delinquency and the improvement in the quality of urban life may be hard to translate into budgetary terms; but public expenditure on traffic could be significantly relieved by the number of people who for health or other reasons would prefer to walk to work or shop if there were pleasant and safe routes by which to do so.

Councils in addition should not forget that their rate-budgets benefit considerably from the creation of parks. The value of leasehold land around Paxton's Birkenhead Park rose in two years following its creation from one to eleven shillings a square yard: the Victorians realised that improvements paid dividends. New York's Central Park resulted in the quadrupling of the rates from the surrounding houses, so that within twenty years not only had the whole cost of the park's land and construction (some $44 million including interest) been recouped, but it was returning in taxes a profit equivalent to half this sum annually.

There are several other sources which can be explored to enable new and improved parks to be built with minimal recourse to the rates. A levy on building development profits either generally in the city or on those parts particularly benefitting from the advent of a park (the means in effect used to create Regent's Park) could be one method. Martin Wagner in 'Stadtische Freiflachenpolitik' argued that the capital costs of new open spaces should be met by landowners, while the maintenance came from taxes. In 1961 New York State started an open-space bond issue of $75 million; Maryland has an instalment purchase plan, whereby the vendor benefits by having his capital gains spread over a number of years, while the state avoids interest on a huge initial capital outlay. Judicious easements and covenants can sometimes bring the public many of the benefits they want over privately owned open land. The best kind of land for parks — hilly, wooded and watery — is fortunately also the worst for building on. Undoubtedly the cheapest way of adding parks is not to destroy the present open spaces we have: it is economic nonsense to erase nature only to recreate it elsewhere at a higher cost.

Several continental cities each year gain a new park after having held flower and horticultural exhibitions, which are laid out on new sites (including some which were derelict) covering up to 3-400 acres in area: various parts of London could acquire a permanent new park in this way if they held the Chelsea Flower Show in their area in turn.

Enlightened businesses might decide that there could be no better form of advertisement for them than to give the public a new park — something both more enduring and more endearing than posters on a hoarding. Philanthropic Trusts and Foundations as well could feel this would be a permanently beneficial way to spend some of their funds, as Andrew Carnegie did when he gave Pittencrieff to Dunfermline. William Whyte estimates that more than half America's parks were donated. Tax concessions could be calibrated to induce more of such gifts, especially in priority areas. Some of the best of the new smaller parks have been provided in this way: in New York the adventure playground at West 67th Street was financed by the Lander

Foundation and the playground on 89th Street by the Astor Foundation. William S. Paley of C.B.S. has given New York $1 million for a park-plaza with locust trees and a waterfall; Bernard Baruch was the anonymous donor of the Chess and Checker House in Central Park. Gifts of accretions, however, should not be accepted uncritically: Huntingdon Hartford's cafe might have intruded disturbingly if it had been allowed to be sited where it was proposed in Central Park.

*   *   *   *   *

ADMINISTRATION
It is difficult to explain to an objective visitor why London's parks are — mainly for historical reasons — split between three different administrations. The table (p138) shows the divided allocation as it was in 1967/8. The central government's *Ministry of Public Building and Works* administers 843 acres of royal park in Edinburgh as well as 5,679 acres in London. Its expert care of every detail of the heavily used Royal Parks — from the formal gardens of Kensington and Hampton Court palaces to the streams running through the plantations in Richmond and Bushey Parks — probably maintains a stan-

Leicester
Square
as it could be

dard consistently higher than that of any other parks department. The public rely on it to plant the 40,000 tulips in front of Buckingham Palace (and in Regent's Park to prune the largest amount of public roses outside Bulgaria) each year; fewer people, perhaps, know that it also has for example to cut the unexpected hayfield of over an acre on the roof of the Admiralty Citadel at the other end of the Mall. Unfortunately the advantage of having a voice in central government, and the fact that its activities can be questioned and discussed in Parliament, failed to save Hyde Park from the Hilton or the new Knightsbridge Barracks.

The G.L.C. Arts and Recreation Committee, before the handover, administered over 5 per cent of the acreage of Greater London. Its parks department had acquired a high reputation, particularly for its provision of entertainment and children's facilities. The standards of the individual London *borough councils,* like those elsewhere in the country, vary.

There are several convincing reasons to support the argument that there should be a single London Parks' Administration, combining the best qualities of the present thirty-five. Such a size of unit alone can offer a career structure which would attract the best staff in this field, and would be able to employ specialists such as landscape architects who are beyond the range of balkanized local councils. Equally, a large unit benefits from economies of scale both in its administration and in planning its plant and tree nurseries, entertainments and children's programmes. The two advantages of more localised administration — neighbourhood involvement and an element of competition between different parks — could be preserved by having a locally elected committee to look after the details of each individual park. These 'consumer' representatives would be able to keep the main strategic administration in touch with needs and experience. A unified parks unit for a large Metropolitan area like New York or London is also able to balance the variety of open space it provides, so that it does not have to cram everything into one local park in the way that a smaller council is tempted to try to do.

The effectiveness of the comprehensive approach can be seen in the fact that 38% of the Ruhr Planning area has been preserved for open space, and that the cities of the Ruhr have eight times as much woodland per head of population as Londoners. In 1940 the five counties surrounding the city of Detroit formed the joint Huron-Clinton Metropolitan Authority to plan and develop the parks around Detroit; a single London Parks' Authority could do the same, particularly for the unused possibilities of the green belt and the Thames. Unfortunately the G.L.C. is at present proceeding in precisely the opposite direction and is handing over more than 130 of its parks to the local borough councils, much to the regret both of planning experts and of several of the local councils themselves — the poorest of which, those who are most in need of parks, being those that are least able to bear their financial burden and which often have the greatest problems in other matters such as housing and welfare.

The planning of open space for housing

103 Park and Botanic Gardens, Melbourne, Australia

estates suffers in many communities from being split between the council's housing and parks departments (instead of being combined, as at Stockholm). Planning, transport, education and finance committees frequently all impinge on parks. In Birmingham the responsibility for recreation was split between the Parks Committee, the Baths Committee, the Education Committee, the Public Libraries Committee and the Museum and Art Gallery Committee. A senior member of one parks' department suggested that another handicap is that the Parks Committee is not always composed of the most active or outstanding councillors. He believes it tends to be used as a training ground and that able councillors soon get moved to other committees.

However local government is reorganised, a move towards larger parks units (combined with the advantages of local involvement) is inevitable in the future, which should see the integrated planning of urban and nearby countryside parks. Hampshire County Council has taken a lead in grouping its various open spaces according to the uses to which they are best suited and planning their improvement accordingly, in order to make the best use of them and to lessen wear and tear. The German cities in the Ruhr long ago formed a Regional Planning Authority to develop comprehensively forest and parkland interlacing the whole conurbation.

Such moves could also help to co-ordinate the public transport which is necessary to help people make use of public parks. Equally it is logical for the cost of parks to be spread over the whole of their catchment area and not to be borne solely by the immediate locality in which they happen to be situated. At present the London and Edinburgh councils are fortunate to have the benefit of their Royal parks free; but other less lucky ratepayers may be carrying the whole burden of a park which is a metropolitan, or even a national, asset because of the accident of its situation lying just within their boundary.

13 Conclusion

In the warmth of a summer like that of 1969 or 1970, parks come into their own. The crowds using them in the heat seemed to have a liberated feeling; the light underneath the trees took on an extraordinary lambency, with opaque shafts of sunlight separating transparent pools of shade.

The more mechanistic our daily lives become, the more congested our towns, ubiquitous our motor cars, polluted our environment — the more likely it is that we will feel a need for the softness of natural landscape. It is predicted that half the people living in Britain over the next thirty years are likely to suffer injury from a motor vehicle; cars in the United States have already killed over two million victims. Yet as countries pronounce themselves civilised, it seems to be assumed to be right that we treat cars better than we do our own bodies: that we spend without questioning several times more on highways for motor traffic than we do on open places for human beings to walk.

For many people, the less apparently planned open spaces are, the better. But thought about them is essential, if only because of their scarcity and the danger that they can be destroyed by those who enjoy them. Britain's population is increasing by the equivalent of the inhabitants of Nottingham annually. American authorities estimate that the demand for recreation is growing by nearly four per cent every year. Unless we expand and improve our parks and open spaces we may end by killing the thing we love; and the paradox is that it will be the best, the most attractive places which are the ones that are likely to be destroyed through over-use first.

To satisfy as many people as possible we will need every kind of park, from wild woods to midtown oases; we are going to need linked networks of traffic-free walks which are pleasant and not tunnels in the ground; we need to integrate the planning of rural and urban amenities; we need our squares and empty sites rescued and put to the best possible uses, catering for the old as well as for children; we need to open up ways for people to take part in sport or art;

and we need opportunities for the inhabitants of neighbourhoods to plan and shape their environment.

Modern aids make all these possible, given the will. But a plan for a park is not fulfilled simply by its being completed and opened: it should be looked at continuously to see if it is providing what is required. Social scientists and lay consumers have their part to play as well as landscape architects if parks are to add to the quality of our lives.

104 Riding in a Copenhagen park

Summary of Main Suggestions

Introduction

1. The popular use of parks is the best way of policing them.

Chapter 1

2. The planning of parks should take account of the needs of the inhabitants of their catchment areas as well as the distribution and location of other local open space. The value of a park is obviously greater if it is close to an area of concentrated living (whether shops, offices, factories or homes) or if it is situated on a busy channel of human movement.

Chapter 2

3. Open space should be planned as an integral part of the urban environment rather than being an afterthought applied like a cosmetic.

Chapter 3

4. Since surveys show that most visitors to parks arrive by foot, their use could be made available to a much wider area of people if public transport services were planned for them. Bus routes around the perimeters of the largest parks should be integrated with radial services.
5. Many more parks and their tennis courts etc. should be lit for use in the evening.
6. Heating and sliding roofs, for cafes, etc, could enable parks to be enjoyed more, particularly by older people in uncertain weather.
7. Neighbourhoods can be encouraged to feel possessive about their local parks by forming a committee to help to look after it. Children could also plant and look after trees.

Chapter 4

8. 'Counter attack' television programmes can help to alert public opinion to threats to their open spaces and amenities.
9. Notices in parks should be reduced to a minimum and their lettering and symbols made simple and pleasant.
10. The function and design of an open space should be planned together but over-planning and over-fussiness can be as harmful as neglect.
11. The design of a park should be made flexible so that it may take account of future changes and needs.
12. Where many different kinds of use have to be catered for, the best plan is to site the more densely used areas on the perimeter so that they can act as filters and leave the centre unspoilt.
13. Few parks in cities would not benefit from having some hills in them which can disguise the boundaries and the surrounding buildings.
14. Railings, barriers and fences should be kept to an absolute minimum.
15. Trees, hillocks and water can be effectively used to screen conflicting uses of areas of open space.
16. Planning should be the servant of people's enjoyment and should never supersede it.
17. Attention to the detail of a design can make or mar it.
18. Materials used should be as natural as possible.

Chapter 5

19. Vigilance is necessary to see that open spaces are not nibbled away by road developments or building.
20. The intrusion and proportions of high buildings round the edges of parks should be particularly carefully watched.
21. The planning of green belt areas should be positive to make sure that they are put to the

best possible use, and not just negatively restrictive.

22. Roads and traffic should as far as possible be kept out of the inside of parks. Where their removal is impossible they should be sunk in cuttings or tunnels.

23. Open spaces should form part of complete traffic free walks across cities.

24. The noise of outside traffic can often be disguised with the sound of running water and fountains.

25. Car parking can be hidden with trees and embankments.

Chapter 6

26. In deterring litter a polite appeal, preferably with a touch of humour, is often more effective than prohibitions which can arouse resentment or act as a challenge.

27. Intelligent planning and durable materials can minimise the temptation for vandals. Badly maintained and dirty property often attracts the most vandalism.

Chapter 7

28. Play is vital to children's development: but facilities for it must be interesting and provide scope for their energy if they are to compete with the interest and excitement of streets. Adventure playgrounds give the most stimulation to many children's imagination. Different aged children require different facilities. Playgrounds should wherever possible be soft-surfaced.

Chapter 8

29. The fullest possible use by the public should be made of the facilities for sport in schools and colleges.

30. Outdoor swimming places could be provided with beaches of sand and also retractable roofs. Some summer paddling pools and tennis courts could be flooded and frozen for ice-skating in the winter.

Chapter 9

31. Parks can be used for bringing the arts to new audiences. Each park might plan an annual festival by and for its neighbourhood. Any profits could go to charities or the encouragement of local arts.

32. Tivoli shows that a popular pleasure park need not be ugly.

Chapter 10

33. In the search for land for new parks, areas held by Government departments, hospitals and prisons in cities should be looked at. Derelict land, and in particular tips and pits have great possibilities. The roofs of buildings can also make small oases and gardens in crowded areas.

34. Disused cemeteries can sometimes be adapted to benefit the living.

35. Experiments should be made in having orchards, woods and farms on land in cities.

36. 'Honeypot' parks will help to siphon off congestion. The planning of countryside and urban parks should be co-ordinated.

Chapter 11

37. Rivers and canals are cities' most wasted asset for amenity. Linear parks could be laid out along their banks.

38. The container revolution presents us with a unique chance to use obsolete docks.

39. Food in parks should offer more choice and imagination, and should be varied according to the season.

Chapter 12

40. New parks could be financed by a levy on building development profits. Philanthropic Foundations and Trusts, and even enlightened advertisers, should be encouraged to donate them.

41. Large unified parks administrations provide the best careers structures for staff, and can employ specialists. These advantages can be combined with neighbourhood involvement by there being a local democratically elected committee which takes an interest in and looks after each park.

Acknowledgements

I would particularly like to thank Tony Southart, David Lee, Sylvia Crowe, J.M. Richards, Terence Bendixson, James Kennedy, John Arlott, Peter Shepheard, John Darbourne, Peter Gatacre, Edward Hyams, Virginia Scaretti and Dr. Edgar Rose, among many others. Also Mrs. Amy Hall and Mrs. Wendy Glynn for their skill in decoding and typing the manuscript, Alastair Service for his encouragement and patience, and my family for their company while visiting many parks.

B.W.

LIST OF ILLUSTRATIONS AND ACKNOWLEDGEMENTS

*All photographs and drawings not acknowledged
separately above are by Kenneth Browne.*

Book designed by Alastair Service.

Table   Summary of total acreage of parks and open spaces mainly within Greater London at 31 December 1968

Acres

| Area | Administered by | | | Total a | Acres per 1,000 population a |
| | GLC | London Boroughs | Ministry of Works | | |
	(1)	(2)	(3)	(4)	(5)
City of London	–	7,189	–	7,189	b
Barking	118	591	–	709	4.2
Barnet	121	1,656	–	1,777	5.6
Bexley	215	1,230	–	1,445	6.7
Brent	–	935	–	935 (965)	3.3 (3.4)
Bromley	288	1,279	–	1,567 (1,643)	5.2 (5.4)
Camden	711	55	134	900	3.9
Croydon	–	2,899	–	2,899 (3,317)	8.8 (10.1)
Ealing	10	1,578	–	1,588	5.3
Enfield	–	1,629	–	1,629	6.1
Greenwich	1,039	205	196	1,440	6.3
Hackney	697	19	–	716	2.9
Hammersmith	303	82	–	385	1.9
Harringey	338	713	–	1,051 (1,121)	4.3 (4.6)
Harrow	–	999	–	999	4.8
Havering	72	1,211	–	1,283	5.1
Hillingdon	–	3,077	–	3,077	13.0

Hounslow	—	1,353	—	1,353	6.6
Islington	44	88	—	132	0.5
Kensington and Chelsea	65	79	20	164	0.8
Kingston upon Thames	—	393	116	509	3.5
Lambeth	512	32	—	544	1.7
Lewisham	625	157	—	782	2.8
Merton	—	1,638	—	1,638	8.9
Newham	10	296	—	306 (293)	1.2 (1.5)
Redbridge	548	546	—	1,094	4.4
Richmond upon Thames	66	1,033	3,912	5,011	28.3
Southwark	340	139	—	479	1.6
Sutton	—	977	—	977	5.9
Tower Hamlets	287	37	—	324	1.7
Waltham Forest	—	558	—	558	2.4
Wandsworth	682	95	233	1,010	3.1
Westminster, City of	13	73	1,074	1,160	4.8
Essex	488	—	—	488	...
Greater London	**7,593**	**32,841**	**5,685**	**46,119**	**5.0 c**
1967	*7,546*	*32,541*	*5,685*	*45,772*	*4.9*
1966	*7,291*	*32,474*	*5,685*	*45,450*	*4.9*

Sources: Administering Authorities

a Figures in brackets include acreage of City of London parks and open spaces within the borough; for details see footnote a of table 10.06.

b Rate not calculated because none of the parks/open space is within the City of London.

c Excluding open spaces outside Greater London (approximately 7,000 acres).

Selected Bibliography

Abercrombie and Forshaw	County of London Plan	Macmillan	1943
Abercrombie, Patrick	Greater London Plan	H.M.S.O.	1944
Allen of Hurtwood, Lady	Planning for Play	Thames & Hudson	1968
Bardi, P. M.	The Tropical Gardens of R. Burle Marx	Colibris Editora Ltda.	1964
Barr, John	Derelict Britain	Pelican	1969
Browne, Kenneth	Clapham Townscape Study	London Borough of Lambeth	1969
Buchanan, Colin	Bath	H.M.S.O.	1969
Chadwick, George F.	The Park and The Town	Architectural Press	1966
Chapman, J. M. & B.	The Life and Times of Baron Haussmann	Weidenfeld and Nicholson	1957
Church, Richard	The Royal Parks of London	H.M.S.O.	1965
Civic Trust	Derelict Land	Civic Trust	1964
Civic Trust	Moving Big Trees	Civic Trust	1966
Civic Trust	A Lea Valley Regional Park	Civic Trust	1964
Colne Valley Working Party	Studies for a Regional Park		1967
Crowe, Sylvia	Tomorrow's Landscape	Architectural Press	1956
Crowe, Sylvia	Garden Design	Country Life	1958
Cullen, Gordon	Townscape	Architectural Press	1965
de Wolfe, I.	The Italian Townscape	Architectural Press	1963
Dower, Michael	The Challenge of Leisure	Civic Trust	1967
Eckbo, Garrett	Landscape for Living	Dodge, New York	1949
Esher, Lord	York	H.M.S.O.	1969
Fairbrother, Nan	New Lives, New Landscapes	Architectural Press	1970
Geddes, Patrick	City Development	Edinburgh	1904
Glass, R., Bennett, H. and Law, S.	Surveys of the Use of Open Space	G.L.C.	1968
G.L.C.	Greater London Development Plan	G.L.C.	1969
Howard, Ebenezer	Garden Cities of Tomorrow	Faber	1951
Hughes, Quentin	Seaport	Lund Humphries	1964

Jacobs, Jane	*The Death and Life of Great American Cities*	Random House	1961
Larwood, Jacob	*The Story of the London Parks*	Chatto & Windus	1881
Lindsay, J. and Hoving T.	*New York City's Parks, Yesterday and Today*	New York	1965
L.C.C.	*Parks for Tomorrow*	L.C.C.	1964
L.C.C.	*London Plan*	L.C.C.	1960
Masson, Georgina	*Italian Gardens*	Thames and Hudson	1961
Mumford, Lewis	*The City in History*	Secker & Warburg	1961
Nairn, Ian, et al.	*Counter Attack*	Architectural Press	1957
Olmsted, F. L.	*Public Parks and the Enlargement of Towns*	Cambridge (Mass.)	1870
Ormos, Imre	*A kerttervézés története és gyakorlata*	Mezogazdasag: Kiado, Budapest	1967
Pinckney, D.	*Napoleon III and the Rebuilding of Paris*	Princetown University Press	1958
Rasmussen, S. E.	*London, the Unique City*	Penguin	1960
Regent's Canal Group	*Regent's Canal – a policy for its Future*		1967
Repton, Humphry	*Observations on the Theory and Practice of Landscape Gardening*	J. Taylor	1803
Rubinstein, David and Speakman, Colin	*Leisure, Transport and the Countryside*	Fabian Society	1969
Saunders, Ann	*Regent's Park*	David & Charles	1969
Sillitoe, K. K.	*Planning for Leisure*	Govt. Social Survey	1969
Silver, Nathan	*Lost New York*	Houghton Mifflin	1967
Stroud, Dorothy	*Capability Brown*	Country Life	1950
Stroud, Dorothy	*Humphry Repton*	Country Life	1962
U.S. Government	*Outdoor Recreation in America*	Washington	1962
Wagner, Martin	*Stadtische Freiflachenpolitik*	Berlin	1915
Whyte, William H.	*The Last Landscape*	Doubleday	1968

INDEX OF PLACES AND PEOPLE

DATE DUE

GAYLORD   PRINTED IN U.S.A.